MYTH AND SOCIETY
IN ATTIC DRAMA

MYTH AND SOCIETY
IN ATTIC DRAMA

By ALAN M. G. LITTLE

1967

OCTAGON BOOKS, INC.

New York

Reprinted 1967

by special arrangement with Columbia University Press

OCTAGON BOOKS, INC.
175 FIFTH AVENUE
NEW YORK, N. Y. 10010

LIBRARY OF CONGRESS CATALOG CARD NUMBER: 67-18774

Printed in U.S.A. by
NOBLE OFFSET PRINTERS, INC.
NEW YORK 3, N. Y.

PREFACE

THE present study is an attempt at putting the two halves of a single picture together—the one half Attic drama, the other Attic society. It is the outcome of a question which probably many others beside myself have been both philistine and sensible enough to ask. Why do people continue to read these plays? As literature they breathe an old world air; they are remote in time, strange in plot, in form unlike the drama of today, and yet they do very definitely and inexplicably move the reader. On the other hand, if they can move us in times like these, must they not have stirred more effectively a contemporary audience?

In answering these questions the first thing to do was to read all the plays through, not haphazardly picking tragedy, then comedy in turn, but in the order of their original appearance as chronological links in a single evolution. The next was to find out how they were produced. The drama *in vacuo* as literature is not complete. It must be visualized, for the imagination, at least, must stalk the boards and come alive again. Here archaeology was of enormous help. A visit in the past to the Dionysiac theater and to the mountain-encircled stage at Delphi did more than volumes to apply the touch of life to the old plays. Further, with all the power of a richly expressive art the Greeks recorded their own impressions of the theater in countless vase paintings, in statuettes and figurines, which are still available in museums or in reproduction. Like small scintillae of ancient life they helped repeople and vivify the ancient stage.

And yet there was something still lacking. As spectacle the plays must have been bright indeed—a moving mass of color and of not too statuesque figures—but the plots, the dialogue, the curious ethical principles involved, continued to seem strange. Was there

here another psychology, like enough to our own to arouse a baffled interest, unlike it enough to raise a deeper question? Could it be that these ancients did not think exactly as we do, or, rather, was their method of expression different? A partial answer was to be found in the theory of the subconscious. Here, then, was non-logical thought emerging into logical, a passage from partly sub-conscious processes into conscious, a contrast plain in the turgid image-making expression of Aeschylus beside that of Euripides, so reduced to fit the leaner girth of a more nervous, more articulate thought.

And the myths—these recurrent myths hammered by frequent use to different meanings—could they have a face value and an-other value too, which changed with the progress of society? The answer eventually became plain. The drama was, like all art, a reflection of society; it was a sounding board on which were struck out discords only to be resolved. That resolution had a social value. It was in Aristotle's term cathartic, or purgative, not only for the individual spectator however, as he imagined, but collectively for the society as a whole. It was a solvent for social conflict.

Thus Attic drama took on a new complexion. It was the expres-sion both of a society and of a psychology—of a society passing from tribal organization into political, from a tribal responsibility directed towards the group into individual equality before the law; of a psychology dependent upon this advance and fashioned by it, emerging from primitive methods of expression into the con-scious use of abstract speech. It became the key not only to a chap-ter in Attic society, but to a chapter also in human thought.

The passage from primitive thinking is an event of importance for the human race paralleled only by the discoveries of the age in which we live ourselves. Since the Greeks it has been in terms of logical thought that civilization has continued to advance. But we stand today in a situation not unlike that of the fifth-century Athenians. Just as they hesitated in that century between the processes of a mythological or primitive speech and a logical or fully conscious speech, so today we hesitate between the older thought which took account only of conscious processes and the newer which takes account both of the subconscious and conscious in evaluating the whole. The counterparts today of Socrates are Pareto and the psychologists.

The history of the ancient stage is traceable over a very long period. A span of some thousand odd years covers its origin in Greece at the end of the sixth century B.C. and its disappearance in a dissolving Roman Empire. But there is one fact which gives a distinct unity to this chapter of theatrical history. During all this long period the theater is closely bound up with that typical form of ancient society, the city-state. It was the city-state which produced the drama, and with it the drama disappeared. It is not possible, however, in this study to carry the story to its conclusion, and for the present this book must remain a prelude to a larger work, the social history of the ancient theater.

Any preface to this book would be incomplete without an expression of thanks to friends for encouragement and criticism —to Harry M. Hubbell and Allardyce Nicoll of Yale University, who read it in manuscript, to William L. Westermann of Columbia University, who helped it find a publisher, and to my colleague Brooks Otis, who read it in proof. My thanks are also due to the officers of the Columbia University Press for the speed and efficiency with which they have handled its publication.

A.M.G.L.

Hobart College, Geneva, N.Y.

October, 1942

CONTENTS

ILLUSTRATIONS

MYTH AND SOCIETY
IN ATTIC DRAMA

Chapter One

MYTHOLOGY AS PRIMITIVE THOUGHT

O F GREEK TRAGEDY it has been recently said that it was one of the functions of Athenian democracy and that in form and content, in growth and decay, it was conditioned by the evolution of the social organism to which it belonged.[1] This sociological view of tragedy is a sign of the times in which we live. It is applicable also to fifth-century comedy, to the whole of Greek or Roman drama, or indeed to drama of any race or climate. It seems surprising that so primary a method has not been applied before now on a broader scale, but the individualism of the past century has been reflected also in its scholarly approach. Until recently the study of the ancient drama has been largely literary, subjective, and conditioned by the views on society in which the critic was reared. It has in general concentrated attention upon the great dramatists as individuals in isolation from their background. For a modern critic it is quite possible to contrast Aeschylus and Euripides without realizing that he is contrasting the generation of one with that of the other. But for the contemporary Aristophanes this was virtually impossible. By presenting the personalities and works of the two before his audience in the *Frogs,* he was holding up the mirror to his fellow Athenians and seeking to revive the group spirit of an earlier, a more vigorous and united, Athens.

The sociological approach, however, is a necessary complement to the literary. It is more objective and with the aid of other sciences can be also just as dynamic. If we had no authors' names to attach to the Attic dramas, nor any knowledge of their myths, we should be forced in grouping them to use the technique of the anthropologist who deals with the art of primitive peoples. The products of such peoples, often the work of superb if unknown craftsmen, are treated by him as part of a group evolution; the recurrent symbolism of a tribeswoman's weaving is interpreted in relation to the life of the tribe. Such symbolism may serve statically as evidence in the history of art, or of the particular tribe in relation to others, but it can become an index of living thought only with the help of another science. To bring the symbol back to life the technique needed is social psychology.

What, then, of the original purpose of the ancient drama, and what was the social function of the Attic dramatist? This was something more than the mere representation of an action. It was the projection of social conflict hidden and disguised from modern eyes beneath the mythological form of primitive thought. To assess the full meaning of the drama for its original audience we must penetrate in two directions—beneath the political framework to the strife of social and economic forces, beneath the primitive expression in myth and symbol to the real concrete meaning. We must, in other words, translate it into the idiom of our own abstract social thinking.

It requires an effort of the imagination to understand the emotional significance of this mythology to its own age. We tend to think of the early dramatist as proceeding in the creation of a masterpiece with a chorus and a plot drawn from old stories like those of Pelops or Oedipus, whose ethical content we rightly reject. But for the purposes of the present study we must try to imagine the tragic tale, the tragic diction, and the tragic form as a vehicle for thought when people had not yet learned to think like ourselves.

It is no accident that the sixth century B.C. saw the rise of the drama or that its birthplace was the city-state of the Greeks. Like the formation of the city-state itself, like the expanding commercialism which accompanied such a formation, like democracy and free speech which resulted from it, the rise of the theater was one symptom in a far-reaching social change-over. It was part of the passage from tribal culture to political life.

This change-over, which has interesting implications for ourselves today, meant a complete reorientation in their existence for the Greeks. It meant the exchange of one order complete with a government, an economy, a society, and a pattern of thought all its own for another radically different in all these aspects. It marked the beginning of what we recognize now as Western civilization. It faced the Greeks with a dilemma similar in many ways to our own, and in effecting the change the theater was one method of readaptation.

The historical basis of the change may be summarized as follows. By about 1000 B.C., that is, some five hundred years earlier, a succession of Indo-European tribes had filtered into the Greek peninsula, established themselves on the sites of earlier civilizations, the Minoan and Mycenaean, and produced a new race. Speaking varieties of the same tongue, separated by the mountain barriers of their rocky land, the newcomers maintained a uniform level of culture. This was the tribal system which they had brought with them modified in the course of years by fixed residence in one place. Actually, life under such a system must have resembled that described in the Homeric poems. Within the tribe the petty chieftain and his leading warriors formed a ruling caste. With the weakening of the chieftains, however, this group tended to become at first an aristocracy and then an oligarchy, riding roughshod over the rights of the common folk. Such is the picture which Hesiod, a century after Homer, contrasts with the earlier period.

The privileges of aristocracy were of two kinds, concrete and undefined. In the first place, the wealth derived from their lands meant for the owners social precedence and a decisive voice in the tribal councils. But concrete privilege was reinforced by a psychological grip upon the community through control of the religious ritual of the tribe, through the fostering of taboos, and through the prominence of noble families in the tribal traditions. The stories of the past among an illiterate but highly imaginative folk were woven into a bright texture of myth, which grew with constant elaboration. Mythology became part of the pattern of tribal thought; it was received uncritically, and, as a result, the tribal leaders, tracing their descent from gods and heroes, moved among their own generation with reflected glory. There thus grew up a body of belief whose importance as a cement for society must not be overlooked; it is worth pausing to examine its social function.[2]

Just as the sharing of a common language makes easier contact between individuals, the possession of a common mythology makes for solidarity within a society. It is almost an extension of language and communication; its figures provide a new range of symbols in human form, and these for primitive man represent a halfway house to abstract thought.

The practical effect of mythology on conduct within the group is as follows. Primitive men, among whom we must count also the Greeks of tribal times, are rather like children in their naïveté, in their narrow range of human association. The child models himself on his parents and is highly responsive to the suggestion of those in his intimate circle; the tribesman adopts the stand-ards of the heroes of his tribe, and is highly responsive to the suggestion of the tribal group. This personal code of behavior is of course more consciously explicit than is that of a child: but for the primitive man, as for the child, it is embodied in personalities, in the actions of his leaders past or present, according as he hears of them in oral tradition or sees them in the life around him. His mind responds uncritically; he is not prepared to weigh individually and abstractly the merits of two courses of conduct. A contrast of the behavior of two characters in the *Iliad* and of the popular reaction to them will make this clear.

The first character is the hero of the epic, Achilles; the other is Thersites, a minor character who makes one brief and inglorious appearance, being represented by Homer rather unjustly as the scum of the earth. In the course of the Trojan War both these men show themselves reluctant to fight, and for selfish reasons. Achilles has been cheated of his concubine, his prize as a hero in war and a mark of his rating in the social scale. The head of the expedition stole her for himself, and Achilles goes on strike. He sulks interminably, rebuffs all advances, and strides out to battle in a fury of anger and guilt only when his inaction has cost the life of his closest friend. Thersites, also, is the victim of his commanding officer's dishonesty. Agamemnon decides to sound out morale among the men and suggests that after ten years of war without success it is time to go home. The leaders expect that the troops will refuse, but Thersites, sick of wasting his time at Troy, thoroughly agrees, says so, and sticks to his opinion. He is as a result reviled and beaten with the approval of his fellow tribesmen. There is no mistaking which of the two shows more courage in expressing his convictions, or that the code of the day saw reason in Achilles' behavior and none in Thersites'. The one had the prestige of a hero to excuse him; the other did as he was told.

The socially compulsive value of a mythology is well known today. In popular movements, where no myth exists, it must be— and is readily—manufactured. With the Greeks, their mythology was grounded in fact, distorted though that fact might be. The story of the war against Troy is more than a historical possibility, as excavations in Troy, Mycenae, and Tiryns have proved. The account of Odysseus' wanderings is a disguised version of actual geographical explorations grouped around one figure. It is likely also that another recurrent feature of the myth, the mysterious curse which hung over princely houses, had its origin in fact; it reflects the darker side of tribal life, the frequent conflict among relatives for leadership which produced tribal vendettas. From the social point of view, however, it was the glorious exploits of the heroes which gave them prestige, and the darker side was kept in the background. But even there it had a psychological value and commanded a sinister respect, for both good and bad in myth were believed, and their mixture helped cement the claims of privilege. Anyone who cares to examine generation by generation the family trees of the two great tragic families, the Labdacidae or Pelopidae, will be appalled at the ethical codes which they reveal. He will find himself confronted with the evidence of a society vastly more primitive than that to which the Athenian plays were presented, and in the repeated dramatization of such tales he will see the influence of an undigested emotional inheritance still restricting in the group the freer use of the mind.

And yet history recalls that such things were not so far away at the beginning of the fifth century. If we are shocked to learn that during the Persian invasion Themistocles sacrificed three Persian youths to Dionysus Omestes, the devourer of raw flesh, the regression to more primitive expression, understandable in a moment of national panic, shows how close such thought was to the mass of the people whose confidence the sacrifice was intended to restore. But it was this same god Dionysus who was also the patron of the drama, and it was Themistocles who in 476 B.C. produced the *Phoenissae* of Phrynichus to commemorate the Persian defeat.[3]

If, then, we may take for granted a partly factual basis for mythology, what is the distinction which separates the mythological expression of the drama from that of the epic or the choral lyric? The answer is in the social development. If the epic utilizes mythology to record the exploits of tribal kingship and the choral lyric those of the aristocracy which came after, tragedy received state recognition under a tyranny, and comedy under a democracy. We will discuss later the implication of these facts, but for the present they are stressed to show that the same mythology was a language which served different masters long and well as the dynamics of thought. Its use in each period, however, was different, and with each social advance its previous service was already done. The tribal kings used mythology to support their dynasties, the aristocracy to enhance their prestige, the tyrant perhaps to reconcile and appease, the democracy to express its conflicts. But with democracy its force was already on the decline. How, then, did democracy come to outgrow it? The answer, I think, is to be found in the drama.

Owing to its mythological form, the subject matter of tragedy has for us a double meaning. It appears on the surface to be the story of the interacting individual lives with which it is concerned. As such it is comprehensible also by individuals in any age in general terms of the conscious mind. But for the more primitive intelligence of the early audience this conscious interest was perhaps surpassed by a symbolic significance more subconscious than conscious. The chief agent for communicating this meaning to the group was itself a group symbol, namely, the chorus. It is the chorus which gives to early Attic drama its peculiar constitution, which shapes its ends, and which binds it to society. It marks Attic drama off in the history of the theater and distinguishes its highly charged religious atmosphere from the other contemporary and historically important form of Greek drama, the secular Sicilian mime. The use of the chorus in the drama was, however, only an extension of the principle of the festival. The Dionysia came to unite the ten Attic tribes which made up the *polis* in a socially harmless competition, a competition of words and thought rather than of action. It was a painless outlet, a sublimation for what we shall see to have been a serious disruptive factor, namely, the strife of economic and kindred groups. In its very form, therefore, the festival was itself dramatic. It was an illusion of conflict, a re-enactment of an earlier struggle. Tribe against tribe, the Athenians competed at the festival on equal terms: from the tribesmen came the members of the rival choruses; to the victorious tribe went the credit of winning. But we find that such is also the use of the chorus within the drama; in the earliest play of Aeschylus, and more obviously in comedy, the strife of group with group dictates the course of the plot. It should not surprise us, therefore, to see the competitive principle at work here also. This was only natural—an organic, almost cellular, extension of the festival idea —and provides a social explanation for the rise of tragedy and comedy.

By a stroke of good luck a chronological cross section of this group mentality throughout the fifth century has been preserved in the Attic plays, made more revealing when in its turbulent period the tragedians are supplemented by Aristophanes. As literature we may deplore the loss of masterpieces by Aeschylus and Sophocles; we may wish that the surviving works of Euripides were less uneven in quality, but sociologically that very unevenness has considerable interest. It reflects a dislocated society; nor is it an accident that in the fifth century Euripides, the rationalist and dramatist, is the forerunner in the fourth century of the philosopher, Plato. The tone of Plato's dialogues is itself dramatic and, though borrowed not from tragedy but from the more realistic Sicilian mime, preserves the organic form and high social purpose of tragedy. Indeed, Plato's own thought remains still a compound of the mythological and the logical. Just as Euripides continued to use the old characters and myths to embody new ideas in visible form upon the stage, Plato, who constructed a system of social philosophy with the use of only one technical term, still had recourse to myth-making to clinch emotionally what his logic had failed to make clear. In the *Phaedo* his arguments on the immortality of the soul derive their support both from the old thought and from the new. Moreover, in giving to his intellectual "ideas" embodiment outside this earth, he demonstrates convincingly the hesitation of his own mind to abandon entirely the demand of personification so strong in mythology.

It is for these reasons that the Athenian drama has a special interest for the history of human thought quite apart from its topical and contemporary meaning to Athens, for it covers a turning point in which were forged the instruments of organized thinking which have controlled the advance of civilization since. This organized thinking was a selective process dependent on adequate terms and definition, which prepared the way for the social philosophy of the fourth century. The process was partly the work of individuals, of philosophers, of sophists and their pupils, but it is the drama which enables us to trace the impact of thought on the people at large. It has been well said by Jaeger in his *Paideia* that

tragedy can be appreciated only if we start with the conviction that it is the highest manifestation of a type of humanity for which art, religion and philosophy still form an indissoluble unity. It is that unity which makes it such a happy experience to study the ways in which the epoch expressed itself and which renders that study far preferable to any history of philosophy, religion or literature alone.[4]

It is also this very element of fusion that makes not only tragedy but the whole drama invaluable for gauging the group mentality of the time. All Athenians were not, like Euripides, Thucydides, and Socrates, men of creative intellect; there were among them many of only average intelligence and prejudices, forming, indeed, a majority to whom the drama is addressed. A dramatist, especially in a state festival, cannot strike too high or too low. His aim is bound to be the mean. He must make himself intelligible. If, as with Aeschylus, his audience of primitive folk is more keenly alive to symbolic thought than to abstraction, it is by visual symbol, by rhythm, by mythology that he can hope to move; if, as with the audience of Euripides, such terms seem quaint, bombastic, and outmoded, then his realistic characters, his everyday iambic speech, must resort to logic-chopping to convince.

But if such are the implications of this approach to the drama —on the one hand social, on the other psychological—it would be hazardous to trace the growth and change of ideas as reflected in mythology without first making clear the social background. The advance of thought in fifth century Athens was rapid, but for the preservation of a changing society its acceleration was essential. What the psychologists have told us of individual mental growth is paralleled also in the growth of the Athenian group. Close knit but still with many of the vestiges of tribal organization, Athens emerged before the Persian wars to complete its evolution into full democracy. After the Persian wars this society proceeded to its extreme; after the Peloponnesian War it was eclipsed in revolution. The rate of progress had been swift. Tribal taboos yielded to political conscience; but, for all the intellectuality of the century at its end, it did not advance quickly enough as the bonds of society loosened. It was Socrates who attempted to harness such speculation to the service of the state, and it is said that he never missed a play of Euripides. But it was Socrates also who in this feverish period turned soberly to examine the words on which men built their thoughts, and it was Plato who was still meditating in the fourth century on the reasons for collapse in the fifth. Thus the Athenian process is the reverse of the modern. Today we are proceeding counterclockwise to a more integrated, less individualistic society. But there is a further difference in the two processes which should also be noted. The Athenians emerged from an inarticulate but coherent group into an articulate but disorganized congeries of individuals. In the process their social coherence, with all the proud confidence it gave a representative like Socrates, was lost. The free *ethos* of the fifth century yielded to the *pathos* of the fourth. The form of thought today is no longer mythological nor our acquiescence in society largely instinctive, as with primitive folk. Events, however, have proved that it might well become so, and a new calculated primitivism emerge again. It is the balance which is important for the future, a balance which combines the solidarity of the group with the free and conscious acquiescence of the individual. Let us turn, therefore, to considering the forms of Attic drama and to the society which they reflect.

Chapter Two

ATTIC DRAMA AND SOCIETY

T HE FIRST historian of the ancient drama is Aristotle, who lived in the century following its creative period. His famous account in the *Poetics* is a sourcebook to which all historians of the theater must turn and for tragedy, at least, has become a canon of dramatic theory. As history, these dry shorthand notes have a more authentic ring than do the dubious rules to which they have given rise. Many dramas have been written to conform with the celebrated Unities, but many others, notably those of Shakespeare, have as successfully disregarded them. Discussion of these rules is at present beside the point, which is rather to emphasize the importance of Aristotle's method, as well as the limitations which his literary point of view and closeness to his subject imposed upon him. This is a necessary brief prelude to restating in general terms the historical framework of the ancient drama, in which the Attic played the predominant but not the only role. Such criticism of his account will help stress those peculiarities of local development which he took for granted as universal, although they were actually conditioned by the society which produced this type of drama.

The chief value of Aristotle's account is, as one would expect, his scientific, biological view of tragedy as an evolution. He regarded it as a growth, knowledge of whose early stages he takes for granted and whose zenith he regards as already passed. In the *Poetics* he confines his remarks to tragedy with only a passing and slighting reference to comedy, which he treated elsewhere in his lost writings and regards as the representation of inferior people.[1] His wish is to classify, to differentiate tragedy from epic, whose mythology it shared; from comedy, its poor workaday relation; from dithyrambic and gnomic poetry which influenced its origins. He writes, however, of the drama with the purely literary approach of one investigating the nature of poetry; he keeps a myopic eye on Athens and is little concerned with dramatic forms elsewhere in the Greek world. Further, as a member of the upper classes, he shows the conditioning of his own society and is reluctant to admit to equal position with tragedy, comedy, the lower-class variant of the same dramatic impulse. It is perhaps this social unawareness which prevented his recognizing that the bourgeois drama of his day, the so-called New Comedy, with its fusion of tragic and comic elements, represented only the life of the upper classes. While aware of the existence of this comedy, he was unaware of its social implications.

The history of the Greek drama has from the start two parallel and important strands. One of these is eastern, Ionian, the product of Attica, and comprises a variety of forms; the other is western, Dorian, the product of Magna Graecia or the Greek colonies in Sicily and Italy, and comprises the mime and its derivatives. The latter is more akin to the drama as we know it, the former had a peculiar development. As long as Greek drama held the boards in Graeco-Roman or Imperial times, tragedy on the stage was the recognizable child of one tradition, and the mime of the other.[2] The development intertwined, as we shall see, and mutual exchange continued for a mutual enrichment.

In the fifth century the Dorian colony, Syracuse, produced in the plays of Epicharmus, Sophron, Deinolochus, and Phormis its own original theater. In the fourth century another Dorian colony, Tarentum, in South Italy, continued the tradition with the so-called Phlyax plays of Rhinthon, a mimic parody of tragedy. The tradition was well grounded, for it was transmitted to the Oscans and through them reached Rome in the following century and influenced Plautus.[3] The chief characteristic of the western mime was its frankly secular tone. It combined parody of mythology with a realistic comedy of everyday life. Its influence extended eastwards to Alexandria during the Hellenistic period, and we find there in the third century the Syracusan Theocritus and Herodas treating the same themes as the earlier Sophron, and Sopater copying Rhinthon. It shows from Epicharmus to imperial times a recurrent typology of its own—women at a festival or practising magic, domestic scenes, mothers-in-law, and jealous women, sketches of the humbler professions. It was frankly crude and popular, and, as far as the fragments allow us to judge, it did not employ a chorus; it originated under the patronage of the Sicilian tyrants.

In Athens also the drama developed under the aegis of a tyrant but on different lines. From the first its atmosphere was religious, and its connection with the city cult close. It was Peisistratus who in 534 B.C instituted the City Dionysia as a folk festival and first produced tragedy. This tragedy was an innovation, and its recognition was next followed by state approval of the satyr play and in 508 B.C. of the dithyrambic song—choral entertainments related in form and belonging to the same cult. It was not until 487 B.C. that comedy received state approval. It is usual to divide the history of comedy into three periods, Old, Middle, and New, and for the purpose of indicating the relationship in time to comedy, we may apply the same terms to tragedy. Old Tragedy is, then, represented by Phrynichus and Aeschylus, Middle by Sophocles, and New by Euripides. Thus the form of Old Comedy which we have in Aristophanes coincides in time with the New Tragedy of Euripides. The political criticism of Old Comedy, however, did not survive the fall of Athens at the end of the cen-

tury. Middle Comedy avoided political topics, borrowed mythological parody and realism from the mime, and, after the death
of Alexander, ushered onto the stage the New Comedy. This was
less comedy than pure drama. It contained strong elements of
Euripidean tragic realism combined with a comedy of manners
which reflected the commercial classes, the bourgeoisie. In a Hellenistic world, where Athens was a byword for culture and a
uniform Greek education was general among the upper classes
from the Fayum to South Russia, the type of Attic life seen in
the New Comedy became an advertisement for Athens as a city
of pleasure and taste, in much the same way as the French farce
has advertised Paris. The broader comic note was taken over by
the now universally popular mime.

The Romans thus inherited from the Hellenistic Greeks an
aristocratic tragedy, a bourgeois comedy, and a popular mime. By
a crossbreed of the last two, Plautus produced his own extremely
lively brand of comedy to suit the Roman society of the time; in
the hands of the Romans, tragedy also took on a vulgar tone. Its
original social purpose was perverted, and it became the background for triumphal processions in which were displayed the
loot of the conquerors. Finally, though tragedy continued to be
played down into Byzantine times, it was the mime which ousted
comedy and carried over the tradition of the Greek theater into
the Middle Ages.

Thus Attic drama underwent many changes. It is time, however, to return to its origins. This question has been the subject
of a lengthy and, to a large measure, inconclusive discussion.[4] It
is variously claimed that tragedy originated in Athens in the
dithyramb, a choral hymn in honor of Dionysus; or in the satyric
play, a burlesque performance of the shaggy followers of the god;
or at Sicyon, in rites to honor a dead king. It is extremely unlikely
that agreement will ever be reached when the evidence is, in the
last analysis, so scanty and conflicting. Notwithstanding, upon
this evidence have been built up hypotheses which rest insecurely
upon the fallacy that one source can be found for so composite a

thing as tragedy, or that elements associated in one festival, dithyramb, satyric play, or tragedy proceeded out of one another, because they had common roots in the worship of one god. The main effort of the theorists has been devoted to tracing from some form of ritual the growth of the thing which became tragedy. Now ritual and the drama are for our present purpose two things apart. We are interested in observing what were the apparent ritual elements in the drama of the Athenians, but the question of the original ritual, if such there was, we must leave to the students of religion to discover. It may perhaps be true that tragedy's form can be reduced to a simple primitive equation, the enactment of a drama of the Year Spirit, who is slaughtered and revives in all his glory, but for our immediate purposes it is irrelevant. We are concerned here with the social functions of the drama, with the use to which it was put in the service of the state, and, if in examining this aspect we should discover valid reasons for its creation, there is a probability that its origin may be thus simply explained.

A recent writer on tragedy, Pohlenz, has expressed the swing away from the ritual explanation of its origin in the following words:

Folklorists and historians of religion have interested themselves in discovering the origins of tragedy and psychoanalysis has not failed to lay bare the discoveries of the Oedipus conflict and initiation rites as its ultimate root. Much that is interesting has been collected, only unfortunately it teaches us very little about tragedy. After close investigation no tragedy has been found to have arisen either in Polynesia or in Central Africa. We must therefore remain within the Greek world if we wish to understand tragedy.[5]

But this is a rather abrupt dismissal. The reason for the failure of such comparative studies is that they do not go far enough. They stop on the periphery. Ritual cannot explain the rise of the Attic drama, because ritual is itself a symptom of society, and unrelated to its underlying framework it is largely meaningless. The ritual element diminishes in Attic drama in proportion as the function of such ritual in contemporary society is reduced. But its very presence indicates in the early period the existence of social forces which have not yet been acclimatized within the new organization of the state. They are hang-overs from the earlier society. It is for this reason that one should insist on what state recognition meant for tragedy, for the satyr play, and for the Dionysiac dithyramb. It meant change from ritual forms to a new status. It meant the beginning of secularization. When the state took over such embryonic dramatic forms of the cult as the satyr play or the dithyramb, it was in reality converting these forms to its own uses. It was taking over the functions of an earlier society, which had expressed itself in such ritual as a means of maintaining solidarity within the group. It substituted for more primitive conceptions founded in uncritical emotion and expressed in mythological terms a freer means of giving vent to social criticism. Such a transition was, of course, only possible after the political advance had been made from tribal organization and the machinery set up for the actual verbalization of society's needs. It is this question mark, this airing of both sides of the matter which differentiates *drama,* or action, with its implication of a free agent, from the passive *dromenon,* or cult drama, with its implication of predestined ritual.

Now the most noticeable fact in the history of Greek tragedy is the gradual secularization of myths which were originally invested with all the religious mystery of belief. Each dramatist, in bringing his myths into line with the state of public credulity and public conscience in his day, is adding his contribution to a destructive process, and if it is certainly right to say with Pohlenz that Greek tragedy begins as an oratorio,[6] it is equally true to say that with Euripides it ends as an indictment of codes which the gods and heroes may hold but which Athenians have outgrown. One cannot lay too much stress upon this fact, for it is the key to the evolution of Greek tragedy. By its aid the sum of what the group accepted as matter for belief became in the course of one century material for the exercise of the individual's judgment.

To understand this process is to grasp the function of the Athenian dramatist. The ideas which Aeschylus puts forward are few but revolutionary in their implications once they were accepted by the whole group; the ideas which Euripides puts forward are too many to be acceptable to all, and are thus impotent in effect. Aeschylus lived and breathed in a changing generation; Euripides lived in seclusion in a disintegrating society, for whom the basis of belief was gone. But it was Aeschylus who first started the process of secularization, and it was he who first introduced the leaven of criticism. By challenging and reënacting the methods of popular belief, he began the divorce of the drama from religion; behind the sacred drama of Eleusis, his birthplace, lay corporate belief in the myths enacted which remained unchanged to the end; behind the dramas of Aeschylus lay the individual's wish to make over in the common interest the inherited belief about the past. Thus drama was one of the psychological firstfruits of democracy. The stage begins to shut out the temple of the god.

Let us turn now to examine the social factors involved in the development of Athenian drama, and trace the change-over of which it is a symptom. The old form of society in Greece may be summarized as follows. Its government was in the hands of tribal patriarchs, the heads of the leading families; its economy was agrarian, with a barter system of exchange; its society was aristocratic; and its pattern of thought, mythological. Two changes came gradually to threaten its completeness: the first was the rise of the city-state, and the second the invention of coinage and the spread of commerce. By the end of the sixth century these causes resulted in a complete split in society, and by a hundred years later, in the substitution of a new social pattern together with a new system of thought.

On their arrival in Greece, the tribes settled in villages, which gradually gave way except in conservative Sparta to a more easily defendable grouping round the foot of a natural citadel or acropolis. Thus arose the city-state. Meanwhile, the use of coinage brought the accumulation of private fortunes and the rise of a new commercial class whose roots were not in the old agrarian system. By the sixth century the antagonism between the older leaders and the new is quite clear in an angry poem of Theognis. "The city is the same," he says, "but its folk have changed. Men who knew neither law nor justice, but wore out goatskins on their ribs and had their lairs like deer outside the city—these men are now nobles." [7] There were two methods of healing this split. Athens adopted one, the way of reconciliation under the law of the city-state. "The ruin of our state," says the conservative reformer, Solon, "will never come by the decree of Zeus. . . . It is the citizens themselves who in their folly and trust in money wish to destroy a mighty city . . . a law-abiding spirit putteth an end to the anger of bitter strife. Under the rule of law there is ever sanity and wisdom among men." [8] The other, a more reactionary solution, was that of the Spartans who forbade their citizens the use of money and set their face against the new social dissolvent.

The political effects of the new economy were not slow to show themselves. Increase of wealth meant also enslavement for debt, and trade and commerce produced a series of revolutions. Popular leaders, called tyrants, used the discontent of the common people to oust the aristocracies and gain power for themselves in the people's name.

As we have seen, it was the tyrant Peisistratus who produced tragedies first at the new City Dionysia, a festival founded by him to consolidate the union of the Attic folk under his rule. In so doing he was carrying on a policy which other tyrants had followed. The debt of the drama to the tyrants was considerable, and it is reasonable to infer that the advantage was mutual. It was Periander, tyrant of Corinth, who patronized the dithyrambic choruses of Arion of Lesbos; it was Cleisthenes of Sicyon who substituted "tragic choruses" in honor of Melanippus for those already in existence to commemorate Adrastus, the hero of his enemies.[9] This he intended as a blow at the Dorian aristocracy, whose tribes he further degraded by the substitution of insulting names. When Peisistratus brought Dionysus into prominence and made tragedy the main attraction of this festival, he was honoring a newcomer in the Olympic pantheon—a god not so much of the old aristocracy as of the common folk, who had worshiped him with rejoicings in their villages. It was from the country district of Icaria that Thespis brought his first performers to the Dionysiac festivals. What was the new policy of which Dionysus was the symbol?

It has been suggested that in the prominence which he gave to the new worship Peisistratus sought a solvent for the old family and tribal cults which, here as at Sicyon, may have impeded the proper knitting together of the political *synoikismos* which was Athens.[10] The same tyrant well knew the credulity of his people, for to secure his own reëntry to Athens after he had been driven into exile, he had had recourse to their naïve belief in the gods. He had secured an exceptionally tall woman to act the part of Athena, and returned in her company, led home by the goddess! [11] If the story is true, it argues a mythological simplicity in the Athenian rustic which was decidedly primitive. As late as the sixth century, however, there were still units within the political framework of the Athenian state who were able to "organize formidable fighting forces and wage private wars in the best style of the Middle Ages." [12] These units were the aristocratic Athenian clans, to break whose power as states within the state it required the combined efforts of the tyrants and of Cleisthenes. Against the power of these aristocratic clans, a revolution was effected by Solon, the tyrants, and Cleisthenes. As Vinogradoff writes, "the ancient Greek state was not conceived as an aggregate of individuals but consisted of clusters of kinsmen, strongly bound together by common interests and common religion, and the earlier ages may be characterized as epochs of federation, the federation of kindreds." [13] The revolution of the sixth century may be thus described as the passage from a disruptive system of tribal organizations to a political system with its power not in the outlying parts, but in the center, as a unified pyramid resting solidly upon the principle of locality.

Solon, the father of Athenian democracy, had attacked the problem, had failed, and had been succeeded by the tyranny, which in its turn yielded place to the reformer Cleisthenes. The most effective reforms of Solon were economic and judicial; politically he was conservative; he relieved his populace of slavery from debt, redistributed land, encouraged trades, freed Athens from monetary dependence on Aegina, gave her a coinage of her own, and set up law courts on the jury system, but he kept the old Ionian arrangements of four tribes, while admitting the lowest populace to a vote in the Ecclesia. He left untouched, moreover, the relative strength of local factions, and failed to reconcile the divergent social and economic interests of Plain, or rich agriculturists; of Hill, or poor pastoralists; of Coast, or the growing power of commerce.

It was Cleisthenes who attempted to centralize the state by an ingenious political system in the creation of ten tribes in which all three interests secured proportional representation. This political success was a step beyond the economic program of Solon, but it must have involved a social reorganization. While the conscious recognition of political control enabled the democracy to

fight wholeheartedly for Athens in the Persian wars under the
leadership of Themistocles, it covered only superficially the conflict involved in the substitution of the democratic idea for the
hegemony of the Eupatrids. What was temporarily put out of the
way to meet the Persian attack came back to the fore as soon as
that danger was over, as is clear in the history of the fifty years
which followed. After the Persian wars, Themistocles disappeared
to become, not unsuitably, a tyrant under the Persian king, and
the Eupatrids reasserted themselves.

Under Cimon there followed a period of pro-Spartan policy
which ended disastrously, owing to the stupidity of the Spartans
themselves. But it was only natural for the Eupatrids to feel sym-
pathy for the aristocratic tribalism of Sparta, and the belief died
hard. We can see in Plato's *Republic* a survival of it. The system
which the Eupatrids so admired was a determined effort to consolidate within an atrophied tribal organization a landowning,
serf-supported aristocracy against an outer world which had developed commerce. It was an effort to preserve an outmoded way
of life of which considerable vestiges still remained also in Athens.
It was the defense of tribalism.

Tribal society, in ancient Greece as elsewhere, has, despite its
variety, certain marked characteristics both social and psychological.[14] It is based on a system of law which operates differently
from that which we know under the same name. First of all, the
primitive code is unwritten; it is not explicit like our own; it rests
upon an elaborate system of coöperation—on a chain of mutual
responsibilities—and, further, it works not only through taboos
which inhibit action, but also constructively and dynamically by
stressing the advantages which follow coöperation between individual and individual, between kinship group and kinship group.
The emphasis on coöperation is achieved through ceremonial,
which symbolically takes the place of written compact and under-
lines the binding force of transaction. Ceremonial also brings
with it public control and criticism, with the result that all the

rules of his tribe, trivial or important, pleasant or unpleasant, are regarded by primitive man with reverence.

What grounds do we have for assuming that these general principles apply also to ancient Greece—that the Athenians at this period shared in a primitive way of life? According to Morgan, in his *Ancient Society,* the Athenians had reached an advanced stage of tribal life in which some of the original features had undergone considerable change.[15] His view that there was a single type of tribal evolution is disputed today, but there is sufficient parallel between Attic and other types of society to show that the Athenians had experienced an evolution which we may describe as from tribal into political life, from that of small units into the life of a larger whole. In some forms of primitive society three main shaping principles are clear. The first is the so-called mother right. Descent within the tribe is traced through the mother and not, as with us, through the father. For such tribesmen all human beings are classifiable as maternal kinsmen or strangers. Next, the tribe is divided by the worship of totems into a number of clans which in turn are divided into an irregular number of subclans. Membership in such implies a common ancestress, unity of kinship, unity of citizenship in a local community, common title to land, and coöperation in many economic and all ceremonial activities.[16] Further, a law of exogamy is established whereby marriage within the clan is forbidden by a taboo of incest. This is known as the classificatory system.

In Athens, before the reforms of Cleisthenes, we find the following tribal organization. There were four traditional Ionian tribes, which were divided into brotherhoods or *phratries,* which in turn included members of clans or *gené.*[17] These clans were closed to all except lineal descendents of a common heroic ancestor and formed the nucleus of a stout conservatism. They maintained their solidarity in the old ceremonial way through common religious rites in honor of their common ancestor, by owning a common burial place and by reciprocal obligations of help, defense, and redress of injuries. In Athens, however, descent was through the male line, intermarriage was permitted within the clan in the case of orphans and heiresses, and children had gained the right to exclusive inheritance of their father's property.

This much is established fact, but there is also evidence in mythology that totemism and, as we shall see, matrilineal descent were not unknown to the Greeks; [18] that operative in the conscience of at least the aristocratic members of the new political state was the old psychology with both its interdependence, its ceremonial observance, and also the inherited system of taboos. At each of the major points of his life the member of such a clan was brought into direct contact with his associates. At birth, at puberty, and after marriage he was formally presented to them at the feast of the brotherhoods, which was called the Apatouria. Within this area the old tribal group life remained intact.

There were, however, many Athenians who could not claim lineal descent from a noble ancestor. For these men parallel group organizations were formed, called the *thiasoi,* and it was a social, as distinct from a political, victory for them when the democratic reformers succeeded in having these included in the brotherhood.[19] From the clans, of course, they continued to be barred.

The function of the dramatic festival becomes clearer if we realize what was the social process of which it was a part. Like the political, the social system had to be expanded to cover a broader base. Just as the old tribal Council, the Areopagus, had been supplanted and its powers taken over by the Council of the new state, so also much in the social organization had become meaningless when the political system changed. The model for reorganization, however, still remained the old tribal group, and the method of publicizing change the old ceremonial one, while the psychology to which it was addressed remained the same, namely mythological, expressing its beliefs in personalized forms, attaching its conceptions to the figures of deities. Thus the festival of the Panathenaea, to which we have referred above, used Athene as a symbol of the new political organization just as the brotherhoods used Apollo Patrous to symbolize the social organization; and by the side of Apollo was now elevated Dionysus, patron of the *thiasos*. Thus the tyrant, in giving such prominence to festivals for Athene and Dionysus, wished in terms of mythological propaganda to emphasize not only the political unity of the Athenians, but also the social—to underline beside the symbol of a folk united under one common rule the recognition also of common birth in the worship of the great god of procreation. It was indeed no accident that Dionysus, patron of the drama, and Athene joined Apollo of the brotherhoods as patrons of their feast.

The social consequences that followed political unity affected both aspects of tribal coherence—both the system of mutual obligation and also the system of taboos. The new political system rendered meaningless the economic purposes of the tribal group; at the same time this undermined the importance of their social reciprocity, but it still left untouched the most lasting area of tribalism, the area of taboos. Reduced as the tribal organization was practically to the meetings of the clans, their members still carried over into political and social life the taboos which formed part of the discipline of the clan. Here was a psychological stronghold which had to be stormed before the democratic process was complete, and this is precisely the function to which we see tragedy bending its energies in the beginning of its history, using the tribal forms, the tribal thought patterns which alone were intelligible to the group, but carrying to the conscience of the people as a whole what had previously been the ethical problems of the tribal clan.

The foregoing sketch of Athenian society has been necessary before approaching the drama itself. But one more aspect of the societal advance must here be stressed in regard to its expression in drama. On the one hand we must not expect the reflection of society in the plays to be direct. Owing to the symbolic and disguised forms of articulation among a group emerging from the primitive, the direct expression will not be considerable; the majority of the evidence will be indirect. On the other hand, we may be pretty sure that the evidence will be there for the following reason. Pareto has shown that there is operative in the formation of human judgment in society a law of "residues" and "derivations," of nonlogical manifestation of sentiments, besides verbal elaborations on them in terms of logical speech; [20] in other and less technical terms, judgments on social issues are frequently determined subconsciously and then elaborated consciously afterwards, a social application which corresponds in the thought processes of the group to the findings of the psychologists with regard to the individual. Thus, in applying this view to the study of Athenian society we may expect to find that, just as considerable vestigial remains of tribal society still flourished in Attica under cover of a fully fledged democratic constitution, so correspondingly there must have survived a weight of nonlogical thought, taking the form of religious taboos, which derived from the older system; indeed, one would expect that, since logical thought was as yet in its infancy and dependent as we have seen on politico-social advance, the preponderance of thought in Attic society must have been of this kind. Thus we may confidently expect that, in so far as the drama accurately reflects society, the earlier section of the drama will be preoccupied with "residues," and the later drama of the century will be devoted to the manufacture of "derivations." And this actually proves to be true, for the progressive secularization to which we have already drawn attention is really nothing more than the liquidation of older attitudes inside society, which, reinforced by inertia and the conservatism of religion, constituted a wall of resistance to a freer and more realistic psychology.

Chapter Three

PRIMITIVE AFTERMATH

WITHIN a horseshoe on the lower slopes of the Acropolis a trial scene is proceeding before the eyes of the Athenian folk in festival assembled. The year is 458 B.C., the festival the City Dionysia. This trial scene is the climax of the *Oresteia,* last and greatest of the Aeschylean trilogies. From the eyes of the people gathered in the sacred precinct's theater the temple of the god is for the time being hidden by a temporary background representing the western entrance to the Acropolis, the Propylaea in its pre-Periclean form. (Compare the headpiece to this chapter with the figure on p. 30.) In front of it is an altar in the center of the orchestra; this represents the open-air court of the Areopagus, the ancient place of tribal trial for homicide. On one side of the altar is the chorus of Athenian elders, the Areopagus itself. Ranged opposite is a chorus of weird sisters, strange figures in costumes contrived by Aeschylus, so terrifying a sight to a primitive audience that on their first appearance these Furies sent part of the audience from their seats in palpable terror. The center of the scene holds three figures, one human, two divine—the defendant Orestes crouching at the altar and Apollo Patrous with Athene Phratria. The leader of the Court has just asked of Apollo concerning Orestes:

> He who poured forth a mother's kindred blood,
> Is he to dwell in Argos, in his father's house?
> How shall he use the shrines the people use,
> How take his share in the clansmen's offering bowl? [1]

For Orestes is on trial for putting into effect that very principle of paternity which we have seen to play a part in the advance of society sketched in the last chapter. He has murdered his mother, Clytemnestra, in revenge for the death of his father Agamemnon at her hands. From Argos he went forth to Delphi, home of Apollo, and from there, at Apollo's command, to Athens to ask aid of Athene. The trial is to decide his fate.

This gathering is highly symbolic. To the Athenian audience Apollo represents visibly Enlightened Religious Conscience; Athene, Attic Law; the leader of the chorus is the spokesman for Attic Public Opinion, represented by the chorus itself; the prosecuting Furies are the Curse which descends on whoever infringes tribal law.

Apollo, replying to the question, urges the paramount claim of the father.

> Not the true parent is the mother's womb
> But rather nurse of the new scattered seed,
> The male is parent, and the woman for the man
> Stranger for stranger, keeps the promise safe
> Of life, unless a god shall it destroy.[2]

The proof which Apollo adduces for this is hardly to our way of thinking a logical one. It is, on the contrary, mythological. He shows as evidence that birth may take place from fathers, without mothers, Athene herself, who sprang fully armed from the head of Zeus. It seems, however, rather illogical that the birth of the motherless daughter from her father's head should be used to prove that the son is descended from his father, and not from his mother also. But the argument has a peculiar emotional rationale, if we remember that Athene was herself a disguised form of the ancient pre-Greek mother goddess, who in Minoan and Mycenaean worship had been supreme, and had stood, perhaps, as symbol of matrilineal society.³ Apollo, then, is carrying that ground of descent one step forward to a paternity principle more powerful than the matrilineal. In casting her vote for acquittal, Athene pronounces

> For what remains mine is the right to judge
> And for Orestes I shall add my vote.
> No mother bore me ever in her womb
> And, save in wedlock never to be mine,
> The male's, the father's cause I do proclaim.⁴

Thus in symbolic form the irrational logic of the argument rehearses before us in brief the development we have already traced in society. The matrilineal principle, Athene, abdicates of her own free will before the patrilineal, for no valid reason that we can logically endorse, but on grounds which had an emotional validity for the Athenian audience of the time. To the conclusion of this play we shall return later.

The scene shifts in time to fifty years later, to the production of the *Orestes* of Euripides in 408 B.C. Again the same situation, not as the climax of a trilogy but of a single play. The background is no longer a temporary makeshift building, but a more permanent construction which bears a remarkable likeness to the splendid entrance to the Acropolis which Mnesicles designed. (Compare the illustration on the next page with the headpiece to Chapter IV.) On this occasion it serves to indicate the portico in front of the royal palace at Argos. Gone, however, are the visible symbolic figures. The Furies are referred to earlier in the play, but merely as the figments of a sickbed imagination. Only at the end of the play does Apollo appear aloft to untie the complexities of the plot. The leader of the chorus of noncommital Argive women

is polite, yet feels herself out of place in the presence of a family quarrel and confines her words to remarking that under the circumstances the lot of a respectable marriage is worth consideration. The disputing parties are all three individuals and represent three generations. Tyndareus, father of the murdered Clytemnestra, is appealing for vengeance on his grandson, Orestes, to Menelaus. Menelaus is brother of Agamemnon and so related to Orestes on his father's side; but he is also husband to the murdered woman's sister, Helen, and so under obligations to Tyndareus.

The grounds of the argument in both plays remain the same. The argument from paternity is voiced by Orestes himself.

My crime is that I killed my mother, but on another count this is no crime. It is vengeance for my father. What should I have done? Set the two counts together. My father begat me. Your daughter brought me forth. She was the field that received another's seed, for without father no child would ever be born. Thus then I argued. I should abide by the author of my being rather than by her who undertook my rearing. Further, your daughter—I am ashamed to call her mother— was involved in a secret and unwise love affair. I will be denouncing myself in thus denouncing her, but I will speak.

And in conclusion after this show of reason, logic, and self-regard,

Happy the life of those mortals who make wise marriages, but those who wed unhappily are unfortunate both without and within their homes.[5]

Thus in both cases the defense and the physiological fallacy on which it is based are the same. But it is society, not the argument, which has changed. In the *Orestes*, Euripides is not rehandling the argument as a traditional one; he is advancing it quite seriously as part of the accepted physiological theory of his time, for we know from Aristotle's *De generatione animalium* that the great Anaxagoras also held this view, and it is on a par with certain of the Hippocratic ideas which are also found in Euripides.[6] In the *Orestes* it is used in a forensic exchange of speeches and was intelligible to the audience. So too was the dramatic setting. The myth has been remolded to express the social groupings, the verbal mannerisms, and the psychology of contemporary life. The figures of the myth group themselves not as tribal kings, but as a recognizable feature of everyday life, the family unit, which had taken the place of the kinship group as the lowest common denominator in society. The principle of kinship is now represented only by the individual males of three generations. The argument is conducted by Orestes in the rhetorical style of an Attic defendant on trial before his peers, reasoned and balanced. Its main theme, the murder charge, has as palliative the rationalization of family and individual reputation.

Fifty years previously the idea of paternity encountered the still existing basis of belief on which the older tribal society had rested. In the time of Aeschylus the notion of physical inheritance from the father and its economic correlative, inheritance of the father's property, could in a slowly moving society arouse an illogical resistance in the audience. The *Eumenides*, last play of a trilogy of conflict, was designed to set the seal of mythological sanction on the new conscious principle of democratic Athenian law as opposed to the old semiconscious obligations of the unwritten tribal code. Politically, in 458 B.C., Athens had already been a democracy for fifty years; judicially, its popular courts had long been in existence, but this very court of the Areopagus before whom Orestes is tried had been originally the court for settlement of tribal vendettas between kinship groups, had then risen to become the Council of aristocratic Athens with powers widely extended, and had recently before the production of the trilogy been reduced again to its original function of a homicide court.

But, if such was the social setting in each case, it is possible also to make out the corresponding differences in the processes of thought. The two instances afford an excellent contrast in the operation of Pareto's theory of residues and derivations in two different milieus, one where thought is predominantly conscious, the other where it is predominantly subconscious. According to Pareto, in the conscious-minded person the residue, or expression of sentiment behind an opinion, is supported by a conscious derivation; that is, the emotional ground is argued on the basis of the less important conscious ground, as in Euripides' *Orestes,* where the desire of the hero to play the part of his father's son and avenge him is rationalized by the argument of his mother's infidelity. In the *Oresteia* of Aeschylus, where the relation of conscious to subconscious thought is reversed, the less conscious principle is argued on the basis of a more important emotional rationale. The thought that the son should cleave to his father is defended with a conspicuous lack of logicality in predominantly symbolical terms.

The foregoing example of contrasted thought processes serves two purposes. It is a demonstration both of the relation of drama to society, and of the change in psychology which accompanies social change. To this extent it clinches the theories advanced in the preceding pages. But it is also a good instance of one method by which we may approach the study of the plays. Two methods lie open. Either we may trace certain recurrent ideas of social importance as they are handled by the dramatists in terms of a changing social background, or we may, on the other hand, follow the chronological order of the surviving plays and find out what are the social ideas with which they deal. The second of the two methods seems the best as a necessary groundwork for a later application of the other. It is not possible within the limits of this study to attempt them both.

It is important before proceeding to a closer examination of the plays to note the relation in time of the four interdependent dramatists who cover the fifth century. Aeschylus was born in 525 B.C. and died in 456 B.C.; Sophocles in 496 B.C., dying in 406 B.C.; while Euripides was born in 480 B.C. and died a few months before Sophocles. Aristophanes, the youngest, lived on into the succeeding century. He was not born until *c.*450 B.C. and died *c.*380 B.C. Thus, between Aeschylus and Sophocles a generation has elapsed, between Sophocles and Euripides half a generation, between Euripides and Aristophanes rather more than a generation. These writers therefore represent the views of men who grew to maturity at well-spaced intervals in the group life of Athens. It is thus to be expected that as individuals they should represent action and reaction towards ideas which affected Attic life, and it may well be no accident that the longest lived and happiest was in all respects Sophocles, whose adolescence saw victory at Salamis and whose death came before the fall of Athens; that the shorter lives of Aeschylus and Aristophanes coincide with the passage of revolutions, in Aeschylus' day from aristocratic society into democratic, and in that of Aristophanes from a democratic to a bourgeois Athens; or that the most precocious of all was Aristophanes who grew up in the brilliant society of Athens at its height.

Aeschylus was not the first of the Athenian tragedians, but of his predecessors what we know is negligible. Little survives of Thespis and Choerilus, who exhibited in 534 B.C. and 524 B.C. respectively, beyond a few titles. Of Pratinas we know that he specialized in satyric plays; of Phrynichus that he was the first to introduce women characters, was fined for producing a topical version of the *Capture of Miletus* by the Persians, and that among the titles of his plays and their tradition are themes which Aeschylus himself rehandled. Thus, the *Egyptians* and the *Daughters of Danaus* must have formed part of a trilogy on the same

theme as the first play of Aeschylus, and the *Phoenician Women*
was a chronicle play on the defeat of Persia like the Aeschylean
Persians. In after days Phrynichus was famed for his martial
lyrics.[7]

Born at Eleusis, Aeschylus exhibited first about the turn of the
century but did not gain the prize till 485 B.C. Between the *Suppliants* (492 B.C.) and the *Persians* (472 B.C.), intervened the struggle with Persia, in which he took part himself. Between the *Persians* and the *Seven against Thebes* (467 B.C.), he visited Syracuse
to restage his play of triumph, and Pohlenz suggests that the
sight of Mt. Aetna and the story of its punished Typhon may have
given him the idea of the *Prometheus* produced probably in 465
B.C.[8] His final triumph was in 458 B.C. with the *Oresteia,* compris-
ing the *Agamemnon, Choephoroe,* and *Eumenides,* after which
he departed to die two years later in Sicily. His epitaph com-
memorated him not as the tragedian, but primarily as the Athenian, the fighter at Marathon, whose ashes rested now far from
the city to whose conceptions he had given such forceful expression.

The seven plays, all that remain of over eighty, belong with the
exception of the *Persians* to the trilogy form. The *Suppliants* was
the first in a group which traced the struggle of the daughters of
Danaus to avoid marriage with the sons of Aegyptus, their cous-
ins. The other plays of the group were the *Egyptians* or *Marriage-
makers* and the *Daughters of Danaus,* followed by a satyr play
on the rape of the nymph, Amymone. The *Seven against Thebes*
came last of a Labdacid trilogy, dealing with three generations of
the house of Oedipus, of which the first two were the *Laius* and
the *Oedipus,* and the third the satyr play the *Sphinx*. The *Chained
Prometheus* was probably the second of a group, which included
first *Prometheus the Firebringer* and ended with *Prometheus
Unchained;* the title of its satyr play is unknown. The *Oresteia* is
a complete trilogy; its pendent satyr drama was the lost *Proteus*.
We have thus arrived finally at the examination of the plays of
Aeschylus, and if the foregoing approach has been sound, we may

expect to find in the new Athenian drama a dynamic use of myth in the interests of the new Athenian state. How then did Aeschylus attempt this task of bringing an older mentality up to date? And how, in using enacted myth as a vehicle for an emerging conscious thought, did he break the inertia of older belief?

In the Aeschylean as in all great drama the conflict is one of principles, and it is in his choice of myth, in his rehandling of the outcome of the conflict that Aeschylus shows the hand of the innovator, for he so contrives that behind each of his trilogies lies a new social principle in opposition to an older. For this purpose the trilogy form was admirably adapted, since it permitted the expression of the following sequence in its three plays, the offense of one principle, the counteroffense of the opponent, and the final reconciliation of both in the final play, the acrid air of dispute fading at last away in the lighthearted buffoonery of the satyr play.[9] Let us examine, therefore, the themes to which he gave a new creative expression and then turn to analyze his method of catharsis.

In the Danaid trilogy, the *Suppliants* opens with the arrival of the daughters of Danaus at Argos to ask protection of Pelasgus the king from their suitors. The king consults with the people of Argos, and the insolent invaders are repulsed. The second play dealt with the return of the Egyptians, the defeat of the Argives, and the capture and forced marriages of the Danaids, who all, however, on the orders of their father murdered their husbands, with the exception of Hypermnestra. The third play contained her trial for disobeying her father and acquittal when Aphrodite herself came to plead her cause. It concluded, like the last play of the *Oresteia,* with propitiatory ceremonies—here for the murdered husbands. Such in brief is the framework of the whole, which serves to explain the—to us—somewhat undramatic nature of the surviving play.

What then is its social content? Here again, as in the last of his trilogies, Aeschylus confronts us with evidence of older codes. The Danaids are fleeing from the horror of an endogamous marriage, from one from which Themis, or time-honored custom,

debars them, even if sanctioned by Egyptian custom. As Ridgeway makes clear, such a plea would have seemed unintelligible
to fourth-century Athenians, for at that time the law permitted
marriage of even half brothers and sisters, provided the mother
was not the same.[10] Moreover, if a man left only a daughter, the
next of kin could claim her in marriage; indeed, even if she were
already married and subsequently became heiress to a family
property through the death of a brother, the next of kin could
break up the marriage and claim her. If married himself, he could
divorce his own wife and marry the heiress. The *Suppliants,* however, gives evidence that the Athenian audience must have felt
that the Danaids had some justice on their side, even if Pelasgus
urges on them that advancement comes from such a marriage.
Otherwise the subject matter of the whole trilogy is lacking in
purpose. The theme points, therefore, to a period when the Athenians could still understand the justice of claims founded in conceptions of a matrilineal society, while they appreciated also the
economic advantages of giving up such ideas. In other words, in
the popular mind at Athens there still was attached an aura of
sanctity to the older system even if the Athenians had for realistic
purposes abandoned its practices. Ridgeway quotes from Justin
and from Varro as preserved in St. Augustine the mythical story
of the transition at Athens from this form of society.[11] It was in
the time of Cecrops, according to Justin, that marriage was established, and, according to Varro, it was the same king who de-
prived women of their votes in the assembly and forced children
to take the father's name and not the mother's. The citizens,
frightened by omens, were called upon to choose their patron
deity; the men voted for Poseidon, the women for Athene, and,
as there was one woman more, Athene prevailed. (One recalls
the judgment scene in the *Oresteia*.) To appease the wrath of
Poseidon, however, the citizens punished their womenfolk with
loss of votes and the right of naming their children after them.

The symbolic significance of the play becomes clearer if we con-
sider the trilogy as a whole. A strife between the supporters of

the older code and those who are seeking to overthrow it invades
the city of Argos, which by giving sanctuary to the weaker party
is involved in the struggle, is shaken by faction, even loses its
king. This, in parable form, is also the story of what had hap-
pened in Athens in the course of the change-over from group
ownership under the tribal system to individual property under
the democratic. The political triumph of democracy was but recent. The constitution of Cleisthenes was in force first in 508 B.C.,
some sixteen years previous to the date of the play; it was the
successor of a tyranny which ended violently but had held in
check the struggle of the landowning aristocracy and the commercial classes. Moreover, the development of the action of the
Suppliants is notable for this emphasis on the strife of groups and
their champions; dramatic action is confined to argument against
a background of dance and song interludes between Danaus and
the chorus, the king and the chorus, then the Herald of Aegyptus
and his group against the Argive king. In the last scene the two
principles and the restraining power of the city state are all present
in the orchestra in symbolic form.

In the *Seven against Thebes* Aeschylus returns to the potential
causes of conflict in the older society, this time in more concrete
form, in the vendetta arising from generations of family troubles.
Laius, warned by Apollo that his son would kill him, disregarded
the warning, but when a child was born exposed him. The child,
Oedipus, was rescued and, returning when full grown to Thebes,
met his father on the way and killed him accidentally, unaware of
the relationship. Arrived at Thebes, he rescued the city from the
Sphinx and married his mother. When the city was visited by a
plague, he was led finally to recognize the enormity of the deed
he had unwittingly committed, and, if we can judge by Sophocles' surviving plays, must in the second play of the Aeschylean
tragedy have cursed his sons, Eteocles and Polyneices. In the *Seven*
Polyneices, who had been driven out of Thebes by his brother,
returns with six other champions to regain the power he had lost.
The usual form of the myth was that these champions were de-

feated, but that in the following generation their descendants, or Epigoni, returned once more and laid waste the city. This, however, is not the ending which Aeschylus gives to the story. He makes both brothers childless, and, on the death of Polyneices, Eteocles goes forth from the city to die as an act of self-devotion, a voluntary termination of the family curse. He thus sacrifices the interests of the family to that of the city-state.[12] Here, therefore, we see Aeschylus handling an idea inherited from the older civilization which haunted his mind and must have been very present in that of his audience, for he returned to it as the basis of the Agamemnon trilogy, giving there a more splendid expression to the liquidation of the Curse. In the *Eumenides,* after the offense of Agamemnon's murder in the first play and the counteroffense of the murder of Clytemnestra and Aegisthus in the second, the final outcome of the trial scene described above is the conversion of the Erinyes, or Avenging Spirits of tribal society, into the kindly Eumenides who dwelt benignly in their sanctuary on the Acropolis, laying aside their anger in return for recognition by the people at large.

This treatment of the family curse, one of the preoccupations of tribal psychology, merges curiously with an evolution in the idea of Zeus in the following *Prometheus* trilogy. It was an audacious conception, indeed, that made this consist, first, of the offense of Prometheus in helping common humanity against the tribal god; then, of the counteroffense of Zeus in punishing Prometheus arrogantly; and, in the final play, of the reconciliation of the two stubborn wills, one human, one divine. If we can see under the mythological form the struggle of social forces, then the undisciplined Zeus is the prototype of an oppressive tribal leadership which was ready enough to preach the doctrine of *hybris,* or the dangers of insolence to the common folk, while reluctant to apply it at home. The unjust Zeus of the trilogy is, however, as Prometheus himself points out, not supreme. Zeus is himself subject to Fate and the Spirits of the Tribe, who avenge the breaking of its taboos. But even Zeus gains by his contrition, for he emerges with extended sovereignty the god not of the tribe but of the new social order, the city-state. In fact, this expansion of Zeus into a universal and moral god is a direct reflection clothed in mythological form of the gain to morality which went with the exchange of an authority divided between tribe and society for the unified authority of city-state law.

As thought, however, such conceptions were not new. They had been uttered before Aeschylus by the original reformer of tribal society—by Solon. What was new in Aeschylus' treatment was his dramatization, his clothing of thought in a visual form which was accessible to the group mentality of the time. Thus, Aeschylus personalizes the divine will whose operation Solon states as a general rule; the one was an imaginative, the other a practical, application. Thus Aeschylus writes:

> Zeus who leadeth to wisdom,
> Zeus who set firm the law for man
> That he by suffering shall learn.[13]

While Solon puts it as follows:

> Thus reckon we mortals, good and bad alike;
> To his own thoughts doth each man cleave,
> Until he suffers. Then he mourns. Before this
> We gape and revel in our empty hopes.[14]

Again, Aeschylus in the *Agamemnon* rephrases more vividly the straightforward thought of Solon. Contrast:

> Old arrogance begets in evil men
> Young arrogance, and at the appointed dawn
> A Spirit bold, unconquerable, unholy [15]

with the following lines from a fragment of Solon:

> Thus comes Zeus' vengeance. Nor like mortal man's
> Is his wrath swift at each ill deed,
> Yet never doth evil heart escape his eye;
> Always in the end the ill-doer is revealed.
> One pays the forfeit now, another after.
> Punishment comes on those who fear his wrath
> With sureness, and the guiltless are punished
> Even the children and their children after them.[16]

Thus Aeschylus is less an elaborator of new and strikingly original lines of thought than an adapter of an old faith to new conditions. With him mythology received a new lease of life, because he put it to dramatic use. It is, therefore, with the garments of this new creative mythology that in the *Persians* he reclothes as drama what was no mythological plot at all, but a recent and triumphant fact, the defeat of Xerxes. It was perhaps the only way in which Aeschylus could have retold the tale, for he recasts this achievement of the city-state in such a way that it takes place among the legends of the men of old. He thus glorifies the city and its people, as mythology had earlier glorified tribal kings and aristocrats, and it is interesting to note how he does it. In place of the mysterious aura of the past and of famous mythical names with which he usually had to deal, he creates out of the rolling Iranian polysyllables and the fascination of a society distant in space, not time, and alien in race a background of awe and wonder; it is a superbly imaginative device, which Milton was to copy under similar conditions, when he sought to revive the Biblical mythology. But even here the mind of Aeschylus continued to move in the channels of Greek myth. To instill the note of doom, he has, here as later in the *Oresteia,* recourse to the spirits of the house, in this case that of Dareius. Indeed, there is a surprising similarity in the development of the *Persians* and in that of the *Agamemnon*—in the gathered elders, in the sense of foreboding before the news of victory or defeat, in the preëminence of a queen, Atossa, who comes forth, like Clytemnestra, to pray, and whose personality overshadows that of the male hero, in the *Persians* Xerxes with his reversal of fortune complete, in the *Agamemnon* the king himself who has yet to pay the penalty of his pride. But this very similarity between the two plays is itself a tribute to the force of mythological expression at the time, for in this contemporary and historical play, the only example of its kind to survive in Greek tragedy, Aeschylus was but interpreting his age, and remolding, as did Herodotus, the facts of history into myth.

With the *Oresteia* and its theme of the victory of the city-state law over tribal codes, we pass into mid-century and to the man who dominates its drama, Sophocles. With this most balanced of the tragedians we find an attitude towards life which once again was consonant with his period, for with the fifty years' interval between the Persian wars and the Peloponnesian there followed a period of reaction and of fusion, of a democracy fairly balanced by a Eupatrid rule which, though shorn of its older power, was still definitely aristocratic, pro-Spartan, and controlled by Cimon. We shall have more to say of this in detail later in treating of the rise of comedy, but it is against a period of balance and nobility that we must place the earlier work of Sophocles, from his first play, the *Triptolemos* to the *Trachiniae*, in which are apparent the beginnings of other influences. It was most decidedly a period of *ethos*, or character, which has found magnificent expression in the red-figured vases of the so-called Fine Style, and it was the aristocrat Cimon who, returning victoriously from Imbros with the bones of Theseus, symbol of a united Attica, decided with his colleagues the disputed dramatic victory in honor of Sophocles. The earliest of his surviving plays is probably the *Ajax*, but the first recorded is the *Antigone* of 441 B.C. The dates of the other five are uncertain, with the exception of the last two, the *Philoctetes* (409 B.C.) and the *Oedipus Coloneus*, produced after his death, which belong rather to the discussion in the next chapter. It is to the *Ajax*, the *Antigone*, the *Oedipus Tyrannus*, the *Electra*, and *Trachiniae* that we now must turn.

In these single plays of Sophocles we may miss the architectonic sweep of the trilogy, but it is replaced by a consummate craftsmanship. Indeed, in the *Oedipus Tyrannus* we may say that the evolving group drama has now approximated, if not even surpassed, the dramatic construction of later writers. The shrinkage of the form corresponds also to a shrinkage in the area of social struggle. The group drama, the trilogy form, has now been succeeded by the drama of a society on which is slowly dawning the consciousness of the individual, not as a solitary unit of society, however, but as the member of a superior group within a larger. It is an aristocratic conception which presupposes a democratic background as a foil for its elevated code. But if we examine in detail the plots of these plays, we find that this code, though that of an aristocratic minority, represents in reality an adaptation of a tribal *ethos.* In his conception of masculine *arete,* and in the conviction with which his women characters act, Sophocles shows us the aftermath of earlier tribal points of view. The *Ajax* demonstrates the new technique. Where Aeschylus had treated the same theme in a trilogy, the *Award of Arms,* the *Thracian Women,* and the *Salaminian Women,* Sophocles concentrates on the figure of Ajax. It is the tragedy of a hero who sacrifices his claim to consideration by his mad act of vengeance when refused the arms of Achilles. He is eventually driven to suicide despite the unselfish succor which Tecmessa offers him. But in this Ajax acts no differently from a Polynesian. Within the tribal code of an unwritten law, says Malinowski,

suicide possesses a distinct legal aspect. . . . It is a means of escape from situations without an issue and the underlying mental attitude is somewhat complex, embracing [as with Ajax] the desire of self punishment, revenge, rehabilitation and sentimental grievance. . . . There is always some sin, crime, or passionate outburst to expiate. . . . Secondly, there is a protest against those who have brought this trespass to light, insulted the culprit in public, forced him into an unbearable situation.[17]

Nor is Antigone other than a tribal heroine in a democratic age. When she insists upon fulfilling "the unwritten laws of heaven" in giving her brother burial, she is not the prototype of the eternal individual rebel against society so much as the weak defender of a code which society has outgrown; she is the eternal conservative, who cherishes the past as something sacred, and will lay down her life for her convictions, for she values, in tribal terms, the meed of ceremonial due to her brother more highly than her own life.

In the *Oedipus,* we see the curious metamorphosis of what was once a pervading tribal taboo, the necessity of exogamy. It is intensified in that the application is peculiarly close—that his sin is one of union with Jocasta, his own mother—but that very intensification, as presented in the case of a man who, like Pericles, was the leader of his people but yet the cause of a plague, is dramatic evidence of the survival in a sublimated form upon the stage of an earlier and more widely spread conception of incest, the haunting terror of all tribal society.

It is instructive to compare the recurrent and pathetic figure of Electra as each dramatist saw it with the eyes of his generation. In the *Choephoroe* of Aeschylus, Electra comes forth from a somber background. After the logically unconvincing recognition, to which we shall return, her individuality is merged in an extraordinarily vivid scene with that of an avenging group. To this also belongs Orestes as well as the chorus of embittered Trojan handmaids biding their time against Clytemnestra. In the *kommos* which follows the recognition with the effect of a rite for exorcising the slaughtered father in his tomb, Electra and Orestes begin with laments born of their weakness, while the chorus spurs them on. But they derive a mounting and self-intoxicating strength from the rhythms of this dervish dance, and at the end, as they advance steeled and on vengeance bent, it is the turn of the chorus to lament. From the action of the group as a whole arises the Curse to work once more; the Spirit of the House, that projection onto ancestral shades of a mob psychology of vengeance, is awake again, a "Fury to spring from the slaughtered and crown one violent end with another." [18] Electra and Orestes are no longer individuals, but instruments of a mob passion.

Not so the Electra of Sophocles. She, like the vigorous Antigone of Sophocles' earlier play, is also given a foil in her weaker, more conventional sister, Chrysothemis. She is not, however, the inspired instrument of a group. She is the true representative of a traditional code which lends her individuality when her sister deserts it. She calls her soul her own, and it is that of a princess, not part of a curse, nor again that of the personally embittered, sexless virago which Euripides makes of the character. She is preoccupied with the ritual of a filial duty; she is exercised that Chrysothemis should attempt to placate their father's shade with Clytemnestra's unholy gifts, and it is on the anguish which she has to undergo in discharge of her duty that Sophocles lays stress, right up to the highly dramatic reversal. Then in the midst of her laments for her brother, her only hope gone, she suddenly recognizes him and her own salvation, but leaves the killing to the men.

In the *Trachiniae* we already see a parallel to the drama of Euripides, whose *Mad Heracles* provides a variant end for the same hero of both dramas. But as Jebb points out, Sophocles, ever the conservative, makes no innovation in the accepted myth such as Euripides has to explain in his prologue.[19] He concentrates on the noble character of the patient wife, Deianeira, the real figure of the piece. If, at the end, in his insistence on the suffering of Heracles he spoils the artistic unity of the whole, the same also is a fault of structure in the play of Euripides. This unexpected lack of artistry, however, may be a symptom of the times, and it is of the disruptive forces already at work in the balance of Attic society that we next must treat.

Chapter Four

DEMOCRATIC SOCIETY

IN THE preceding discussion of Attic drama little space has
so far been given to tragedy's social counterpart and rival,
comedy. Indeed, it is usual to treat separately the rise and
fall of the two forms. This is for our present purpose impossible,
however, since both are facets of the same society and variants
of the same dramatic impulse. We must pause, therefore, before
entering the period of the Peloponnesian War, when democracy
had attained its full power, to examine briefly both the antecedents
and aims of this more typically democratic form of the drama.
For, though originally distinct and opposed in their social outlook, it is during the war that the complementary nature of
tragedy and comedy becomes clear; for we have arrived, as it
were, at a disputed realm in which two men of differing temper-
ament are rivals in social criticism and at an age to which as a
whole we may well apply an epithet of the old comedian, Cratinus, and dub it "Euripidaristophanic." [1]

As already pointed out, the rise of comedy came much later
than that of its rival, official sanction being given nearly half a
century after Peisistratus first produced tragedy. The date of that
public recognition, 487 B.C., came in a lull between national crises.

After Marathon, before Salamis, the leadership of the people suddenly changed. It slipped from the hands of aristocratic Whigs into those of a popular leader. It passed from the progressive Alcmaeonids to Themistocles, who was in effect at this period an *ad hoc* tyrannus within the democratic system. Since at Marathon the Alcmaeonids had been suspected of pro-Persian treachery, their political eclipse removed for the time being a buffer between the rival forces within the state, each of whom emerged stronger from the first defeat of the Persians. For after Marathon the morale of the people had justly risen, while, on the other hand, the party of the landowning families had also gained prestige from the able generalship of Miltiades. When, therefore, after Salamis the Persians had been driven from the Aegean but had still to be kept at bay, this party felt strong enough to assert its power, and Themistocles rapidly disappeared. But since in due course it too was discredited, the middle party, which had revived in the interval, came forward once more to temper with Pericles the wind of democracy. Once again the same family which had given Athens its constitution set the tone for the state—for a gentleman's republic—democratic, indeed, but led by an aristocrat. Like Themistocles before him, the opposition leader, one Thucydides, was removed, and not until Pericles was dead and the Peloponnesian War let loose, did the rising wind become under Cleon's star a gale.

Thus, in the days before Salamis, when there was need of harmony within the *polis*, it may well have been sound political wisdom to sanction a state-controlled expression of popular sentiment and to permit the new comic chorus to take its place beside the now dignified performers of aristocratic tragedy. But if tragedy, as Aristotle says, took its time in achieving dignity, dignity was never during this period the keynote of comedy, whose social catharsis in the fifth century always took more direct and outspoken form than could ever that of tragedy. We know little of early comedy except a few names, a few titles, and some unsatisfactory fragments, but in a notice from Plutarch's *Glory of the Athenians* we mark a pre-Aristotelian disdain already working against it.[2] Conservative opinion—that of the Areopagites again—was opposed to comedy. Indeed, "they considered it so undignified and vulgar that a law was passed forbidding any of their number to write it." Further, in 440 B.C. the law of Morychides attempted for three years to muzzle its presonal criticism, though unsuccessfully, for the law was repealed. By 425 B.C., however, the date of the Acharnians, times had changed, and at this juncture after sixty odd years the shafts of Aristophanes' first surviving play were aimed not any longer at a defensive aristocracy, but full and square at Demos himself and the leaders whom he had chosen.

What, then, was in a fully democratic state the social function of the drama, of both tragedy and comedy? Was it the same as that of tragedy in earlier times, as with Aeschylus or with Sophocles? Further, was it the same for both tragedy and comedy? It will be clear, I think, in what follows that the function of the drama had not altered and that the need for a ventilating criticism was, indeed, if anything, more urgent than ever. But if the need of criticism remained the same, the material for criticism did not, since the problems of society were by now utterly different. For if in Aeschylus, as we have seen, tragedy performed a social service by illuminating the misty mentality of the Eupatrid domination, if in Sophocles it had become a makeweight presentation of the dignified codes of a powerful minority, by the time of the Peloponnesian War such functions were nearly completed. So far as tragedy had been used to combat residual modes of tribal thought or to bolster in the face of democracy the codes of the aristocrat, such matter for conflict was now mostly over and done with. More insistent were the problems of the hour, the outcome of a war-torn democracy. It thus became more necessary than ever to preserve the precarious balance of society, and as aids to such stabilization both tragedy and comedy had related functions to fulfill.

But if their ultimate purpose was the same, the two dramas

attacked their problems from widely separated points of view.
Both felt increasingly the need of realism and innovation, but
the spirit of comedy was younger, fresher, more forward-looking,
and its expression more realistic; the spirit of tragedy more closely
bound to the past, more constrained by convention, its medium
somewhat outmoded. This contrast is clear in their variant use
of mythology. For with tragedy mythology was of its very es-
sence. It was both the source of plot and its interpretation an
end in itself: with comedy, on the other hand, it became in large
measure a source of parody. Thus we find Euripides hampered
from the start in achieving realism by the weird nature of his
conventional plots, while for Aristophanes, from his first play
forward, the grandiloquent unreality of tragedy was an inexhaustible storehouse of fun.

But here again, before we examine the two forms of drama
in parallel, a preliminary word must be said of the peculiarities
of comedy itself. For the exuberant vigor of comedy is due in
part to its youth, and its contrast with tragedy to the fact that in
Aristophanes we are matching the development of an Old Comedy
that had yet far to go with what was already reaching in Euripides its final form in the New Tragedy. We must expect,
therefore, that formally, as drama, tragedy had much to teach
its younger rival, and, indeed, the structural analogies with contemporary tragedy may be plainly seen in the comedies. But, at
the same time, beneath a formal approximation the more primitive form is also present even at this late date, and with Aristophanes it is easier to trace the same process which we have already
observed in tragedy, namely, its rise out of a festival and processional form and its gradual modification for social uses. Thus,
just as tragedy developed from the sublimation of group conflict
with the predominant chorus as its symbol, so comedy, too, bears
the mark of its origin. If with Euripides the use of the chorus
is now different from its primitive role and rather superfluous
to an action that now centers on individuals, in the younger

drama, on the other hand, the chorus is still vastly important, and revives in new form the conflict of groups or, more accurately perhaps, of group and individual. Here, too, as earlier in tragedy, the chorus is the medium for expressing the conflict.

It has been shown by Zielinski that within the plays of Aristophanes is clearly traceable a dramatic nucleus, a processional sequence which goes far to amplify Aristotle's meager account of its origin; for, when Aristotle informs us that comedy originated with the leaders of the phallic songs and was the spontaneous creation of volunteers, this brief notice of its festival origin can be further extended.[3] The result then presents us with a formula for structure in which the variables of subject and presentation are supplied by the needs of society. The usual structure of an Aristophanic play has been summarized thus:

In the prologue the revolutionary designs of the hero are explained, and he is about to materialize them, when the chorus enters and opposition develops. The feelings of this group are expressed in a short sequence, (or *syzygy*) on their entrance; a second sequence contains their murderous threats against the hero, his pleas that they listen to reason and the final acquiescence of the chorus or the character who pleads their cause. Then comes a debate—the *agon* or conflict—in which the opposed opinions are rationally tested and the revolutionary one is found to be the better. The opposition is now over and the new order becomes a *fait accompli*.[4]

The chorus now deliver the *parabasis,* or short, hard-hitting speech generally of political and social application, followed by two sequences in which the results of the revolution are presented. The play concludes amid general rejoicing after either a less vigorous renewal of the struggle or a second speech of advice. I think it is pertinent here to observe that in such a form we have again, as in tragedy, a repetition in miniature dramatic form of a larger process, for just as early tragedy reënacted the strife of rival factions and the conflicts of tribal society, so here we have a representation of the democratic process at work, and of a victory dependent upon argument and conviction such as was needed to secure the passage of a law in the Assembly.

If, then, we compare the functions of tragedy and comedy, we find that, while both are the expression of conflict within the group, the first is of group within group and the second of an innovating individual who gathers a minority to win by persuasion. Thus, in their order the plays of Aristophanes are built around the following ideas: a peace offensive led by an individual (*Acharnians,* 425 B.C.); an attack on Cleon led by an individual (*Knights,* 424 B.C.); an attack by one of its victims on the new sophistic education (*Clouds,* 423 B.C.); an attack on the jury system (*Wasps,* 422 B.C.); an attack on war profiteers (*Peace,* 421 B.C.); a revolt of individuals against Athenian society and an attempt at a Utopia (*Birds,* 414 B.C.); a sex strike led by individual women to secure peace (*Lysistrata,* 411 B.C.); and, conversely, an attack by the same women on their supposed foe but real champion, Euripides (*Women at the Thesmophoria,* 411 B.C.); and in his last play before the fall of Athens, the *Frogs* of 405 B.C., a strife between individual poets, Aeschylus and Euripides, to claim leadership of a falling city. The remaining two plays belong to a changed society and need not concern us here.

Thus, at the first glance, the subject matter of comedy is preeminently realistic and everyday. On a lower level than tragedy, its objectives are mundane—greater comfort in life and better economic conditions are its chief concern. It is little concerned with scruples of conscience or the conflict of ethical codes. Nor did it need any mythology to express its aims. This is not to say, however, that it did not make use of mythological figures. On the contrary, it invested some mythological figures with a character all its own. Chief among these are Heracles, whom it made a greedy but amusing lout, Dionysus its mincing weakling, Odysseus its dearly loved knave, and the Cyclops its one-eyed figure of fun. Time and again these popular figures appear both in terra-cotta statuettes and in the plays in contrast to their tragic selves.[5] Indeed, comedy was only too ready to represent the gods

at a disadvantage as in the *Birds,* or in the *Peace,* and its mythological freedom is in clear contrast to that of the New Tragedy,
to which we at last must turn.

The form of tragedy with Euripides received from his predecessors was already far removed from the symbolic group drama
from which it sprang. If we take the evolution of the chorus
as indicative of the change, then, indeed, the importance of the
original group had yielded to the play of individual characters,
for Sophocles with a dramatic instinct responsive to his times had
added a third actor to the already existing two for precisely this
purpose. But the chorus in Sophocles, as has often been pointed
out, performs the role of a sympathetic and ideal spectator in a
more properly integrated relationship to both actors and audience
than in either of the other dramatists. Here again, this balance
is evidence of a harmonious society such as Euripides seems not
to have known. For him the chorus was at moments an incon-
venient legacy that went with the form and impeded the satis-
factory outcome of the new plots of suspense which he was de-
vising out of mythology. This shift in plot, this concentration on
the fortunes of the individual, is the most significant social feature in the New Tragedy. It is for this reason that Aristotle called
its poet the most human of the tragedians, since it is with the
fate of the individual that he came to be most concerned, sharing in this the outlook of New Comedy and anticipating the
prevalent note of Hellenism. In the more realistic atmosphere of
his theater the chorus, when it did not interfere with the privacy
so essential for the designs of his characters, as for example in the
Ion where it reveals a secret plot unfolded in its hearing, can be
on occasion an encumbrance, as in the *Iphigeneia in Tauris.* There
it is stranded on the beach after the main characters are rescued,
and resembles the baggage which is forgotten on the quay in
the haste of departure and then suddenly remembered. A more
effective function, however, is its use as an interlude, a lyric
relief between the acts of a gradually articulated five-act drama.
Here again, its purpose is now crystallized out of that of its origi-

nal state, and the mood is frequently a relief from a contrasting atmosphere of sensational and terrific plot. The beauty of the lyrics can be matched in a similar setting in Aristophanes.

Something has already been said of that parody of tragedy which so delighted Aristophanes. More than traces of the same can also be found in Euripides, though in a slightly modified vein. In the *Electra* and the *Ion* this takes different form. In the first it is directed against the previous method of tragic presentation, in the second, against the subject matter and tone of the old mythological plot. In both this is a sign of a changed mentality in the age.

In the *Electra* the recognition scene, whose handling is one of the connecting links between the three dramatists, is a deliberate parody of Aeschylus.[6] The oldest example was accomplished before an audience only too ready to believe the visual evidence— a lock of hair, a footprint, and a robe which Orestes had taken away in childhood, regardless of the fact that brothers and sisters need not have the same color of hair, or the same size in shoes, or that Orestes would still use the same robe. The illogicality of the proof struck also the generation of Euripides, for when the old man in his play comes to Electra with the news that at Agamemnon's grave he had found "locks of auburn hair," and urges her to match them with her own, she replies with cold logic "Your words are unworthy of a man of sense. . . . How should our hair match? The clue is useless." Undaunted, the old man, typical of an older and more credulous generation, urges her to put her foot in the print of his shoe. To which she replies: "How could a foot make an imprint on stony ground? Even if it did, the foot of brother and sister would not be the same in size, for a man's is larger." There is no convincing this too acute brain. Yet he tries again, slightly disappointed at the lack of faith in one who should have been only full of expectant trust. "Have you no means, in case your brother should come, to recognize the weaving of your loom, the robe in which I rescued him from death?" But Electra is hopeless. She rejects even this. "Do you not remember that I was still a baby when Orestes left the country? Even if I had woven him a robe, how could he, a mere child at the time, still be wearing the same, unless [a final touch of ridicule] clothes and bodies grow together?" The old man gives up. He has, finally, like an old slave in New Comedy, to resort to a scar, which he recognizes when Orestes arrives.

In the *Ion,* which we will treat later in its relation to Menander, the obvious dissatisfaction of Euripides with the legacy of mythology is most conspicuous of all, for the misfortunes of his characters are not even traceable to the goddess Chance, but to a cowardly Apollo, who certainly forfeits his role as the embodiment of an Enlightened Religious Conscience. He deceives first Creousa, then Xuthus her husband, and finally runs away from facing the fruit of his misdeeds, the hero Ion, who, ancestor though he was of the whole Ionian race, is in this play only Apollo's bastard.

It is safe to say that with Euripides mythology is sometimes more the obstacle to thought than it is a vehicle for it. But as an inexhaustible storehouse of sensational plot it was rich indeed. He draws from it at times somewhat after the manner of the writers of the satyr play and for the same purposes—for novelty and for escape. Thus the *Alcestis,* the first surviving play, was based on a theme treated before as a tragedy by Phrynichus, but handled by Euripides to take the place of a satyr play. Beside the tragic theme he introduces an admixture of the comic characteristics of Heracles; in the *Helen* he converts the plot of the *Proteus* of Aeschylus into a drama of phantasy. Where Aeschylus, by contrasting the adventures of Menelaus in Egypt, had given relief after the *Oresteia* and the tragic story of Agamemnon, Euripides developed the theme into one of his familiar plays of suspense, with a happy ending. It belongs to the period of the Sicilian expedition, and, like the *Andromeda* or the *Iphigeneia in Tauris,* offset the air of tragedy too frequently present in

Athens during the war; the happy outcome, the setting in distant lands, are matched by the contemporary Cloudcuckooland of Aristophanes' *Birds*.

Three distinct periods may be made out in the chronology of the Euripidean plays, corresponding with the years before the outbreak of the Peloponnesian War, the first ten undecisive years of that struggle, and the final declension of democracy as the century ended. Even in the first period, however, there are already clear certain social preoccupations which are intensified with the progress of events and may be interpreted as a symptomatic response to the temper of his audience during this painful period. In part they are the product of a rampant and excessive individualism which accompanied democratic rule, but they are evidence of a split in the coherence of society, revealing, as they do, a focused and articulate realism alternating with a blurred and inarticulate *Weltschmerz*. Superficial judgment has often attributed to Euripides the individual this choice of exotic theme and to the contemplative solitary in his Salaminian cave, to the bookish possessor of the first recorded library, the morbid or escapist nature of his plots. The fissures, however, of which these trends are evidence, run deeper than the mind of the dramatist; they penetrate the fabric of society, as Aristophanes was well aware. Although his laughter may seek to deprecate the depleted tone of the age and to pillory Euripides for emphasizing the truth, the comic as well as the tragic poet was troubled by the same phenomena. Even the unflinching aristocratic code of Sophocles felt in this period of war the impact of the change. His Neoptolemus in the *Philoctetes* is an aristocrat who, like Alcibiades, serves an unworthy master, the wily Odysseus, symbol of Demos. Perhaps Sophocles felt that there was no longer room in Athens for nobility and was conscious of uttering in his last play its swan song, for Oedipus comes to Colonus, cursing his children, to die, and only by his own death does he confer a blessing.

To the first period belong the *Alcestis* (438 B.C.) and the *Medea*

(431 B.C.), which have survived, the *Alcmaeon* and *Telephus* (both 438 B.C.) and the *Philoctetes* (431 B.C.), which have not. Already in his first play, the *Daughters of Pelias* (455 B.C.), Euripides had struck out into the bypaths of sensational myth as a background for his drama of the individual. He did so with a purpose, for he was already concerned with the position of women in a democratic Athens, with the outcome of that social revolution which we have traced in the previous chapters. Nowhere else did society possess more explosive material than in these voiceless sufferers under democracy and the strain of war. But they needed leadership. Thus, just as Aristophanes at the century's end aired in the *Lysistrata* the rising revolt of the women, Euripides raised the standard with Medea. As a fascinating oriental princess, she is a foil for such innocent victims of male arrogance as Alcestis shows herself to be. In both cases the splendid character of the women is in marked contrast to the self-seeking priggishness of their husbands. As dramatist, however, he sought novelty at every turn to please his restless audience. Of Alcmaeon he made a romantic hero, seeking in that victim of tribal codes a variant for Orestes. This was but a step further in the process of sentimentalizing the myth. By way of contrast, in the *Telephus* it was the extreme realism of the treatment which startled the audience. The sight of the mythical prince in rags made a lasting impression on Aristophanes, who, sensing perhaps an invasion of his own sphere, never ceased to use the play for parodic episodes.

The early war plays, the *Hippolytus* (428 B.C.), the *Hecuba* (425 B.C.), and the possibly contemporary *Andromache* show a clearly embittered note in the insane passions of these women, either betraying or betrayed. Besides them, a patriotic note is struck in the *Heracleidae* (422 B.C.), the *Suppliants,* and the *Mad Heracles* (420 B.C.), for the figure of Theseus emerges as an Athenian man of good will in the midst of distress and the slaughter of innocence. Once more the theme of a helpless victim is insistent—in the death of Macaria, the suttee of Evadne, and

in the murder of Heracles' own children. This was a theme of which the humanitarian in wartime never tired.

In the last period bitterness and escapism alternate. The parody of the *Ion* (415 B.C.) is as disillusioned as is the picture of war's desolation in the *Troades* of the same year. These plays followed close on the destruction of the defenseless Melians. Escape was necessary for sanity, and it came in the *Alexander,* a romantic picture of a pastoral prince. But in the *Palamedes,* on the other hand, we have the just man victim of his oppressors, followed in the period of the Sicilian expedition by the *Iphigeneia in Tauris,* the *Helen,* and *Andromeda,* plots of faraway lands and successful undertakings.

In contrast, the *Electra* of 413 B.C. shows a confused and harried society leveled by the war. The emotionally torn heroine is a princess degraded in an unconsummated *mésalliance* with an impoverished bourgeois. Again, in the *Phoenissae* of 410 B.C. we have the slaughter of innocents, of children sacrificed to the interest of parents, Mcnoeceus to those of Creon, Iphigeneia in the Aulid play to those of her father Agamemnon; even in the *Bacchae* Pentheus is rent in pieces by Agave, his mother. The temper of the times is well reflected in the increasing violence with which Orestes, male counterpart to Electra, is depicted—delusional in the *Iphigeneia in Tauris,* in the play named after him a maniacal gangster. Athens, Euripides seems to say, is justified in her children, for some she slaughters and others she drives to madness. There is at this point no mistaking the realistic message of the myth. Not here the conflict of tribal society and city-state, nor of aristocratic code and democratic interest. This was the conflict of the human soul in the shattered ruins of a society.

Chapter Five

BOURGEOIS SOCIETY

AFTER the fourth century we enter upon a new world. Between the battle of Chaeroneia in 338 B.C. and the death of Alexander in 323 B.C. the outlook for the Greek city-state changed for good. It was the irony of fate that Aristotle, who saw in the city the ultimate norm of human civilization, should have been the tutor of the very man who helped destroy its political freedom. But here again, despite a political decline the social values of the system continued to live on; for Alexander and his successors, like the Romans after them, realized the value of the city-state unit as a nucleus of civilization in the midst of less civilized areas, and by the creation of such colonies throughout the huge new area open to Greek influence, from Macedon to India, from the Black Sea to the cataracts of the Nile, sought to perpetuate its social benefits.

The source of inspiration both in the theater and in the new literature now shifted with a change of patronage. The forms of the drama took on a more universal tone, calculated on the one hand in New Comedy to appeal to an educated and standardized public of scattered Greeks, on the other to a frankly popular taste in the mime.[1] Hellenistic Athens, basking in the reflected glory of its earlier centuries, became a city of pleasure and education— a mixture of *ville lumière* and university town, where famous courtesan and famous philosopher jostled on the street—while the products of its theater were copied, its techniques imitated, by traveling companies of actors, the celebrated Dionysiac artists, throughout the Hellenistic world. The society to whom this theater appealed must be briefly sketched, for one considerable section of its public may be roughly grouped under the name of a bourgeoisie, a privileged class into whose ranks entrance could be gained only by the adoption of a Greek education. The highest classes in the Hellenistic cities spoke Greek, the *koine* or a standard Attic; their life centered round the palaestra and gymnasium; the books they read were Greek.

The Hellenistic period was, moreover, one of great economic development. The kings of the heterogeneous kingdoms proceeded to the exploitation of their resources with the assistance of Greek science and of well-trained Greek minds. Trade, encouraged by the opening up of new areas, was kept in constant circulation, and the known world became one huge market controlled by the Hellenized merchant and the Greek middleman. Banking on a scale undreamt of by the celebrated Pasion of fourth century Athens developed; monetary systems adapted themselves to one another to facilitate exchange. Important trading centers like Delos came to know an international, cosmopolitan life.

To take charge of this trade there grew up in the cities a vast wealthy middle class, a fairly mobile population if contrasted with the settled populations whose products they exploited. There appeared also at the same time a sharp cleavage between the exploiting class and those whom they exploited. While luxury developed, as is clear from the evidence of Hellenistic bourgeois houses, and rich men could be found to carry the burden of municipal expenditures for extraordinary projects, wealth tended to concentrate in the cities. The city population absorbed the products of industry, which was geared to the needs of Hellenized city life, and there arose gradually a proletariat of consumers. Industry was carried on for the benefit of a small number, as the factories were small and the work of slaves the substitute for our modern machinery. On the other hand, the flow of gold, which Alexander had first let loose upon the Greek world, produced a depreciation in the value of money, and prices rose. Food and the necessities of life became more expensive, and social unrest began. In a community like Delos the wages of unskilled free labor, replaceable by groups of slaves, could not rise above the slave rate and sometimes fell below it. The gap, on the other hand, between rich and poor continued to grow greater. In the cities the clause preventing redistribution of land or cancellation of debt becomes more frequent in the inscriptions, and the protection afforded by the Macedonian kings to the League of Cities takes on a social as well as a political aspect. Elsewhere, the Hellenistic communities lived continually on the verge of revolution. In Sparta, where wealth had now concentrated in the hands of heiresses, it broke out in 244 B.C. Agis IV attempted a popular socialistic reorganization of what had originally been an aristocratic tribal state. Though he failed, the attempt was repeated by Cleomenes III, only to be suppressed by the Macedonians.

In the midst of considerable prosperity an insecurity invaded daily life. The recurrent wars between the Hellenistic kingdoms and the growth of piracy left few certain of wealth or the undisturbed possession of their rights as free men. If captured, they might easily be sold into slavery. In the fluctuating population of these commercial cities, the Greek trader became *déraciné* and turned to other substitutes for the older city-state discipline. The goddess he most favored was *Tyche* or Chance, and he sought an outlet for his social instincts in clubs and societies—in *thiasoi*, or religious groupings connected with the worship of a particular deity; in *eranoi*, or friendly societies; in professional associations. In Delos we find, for example, the clubhouse of the Berytian merchants with a shrine for worship of their own native gods, or that of the Poseidoniasts with hotel quarters and club privileges. Better educated men found a bond in following the universalized philosophies such as Stoicism or Epicureanism. Indeed, it is in the social writings of such philosophers as Bion the Borysthenite, Cercidas of Megalopolis, and Phoenix of Colophon that criticism of the inequalities of wealth soon took expression.

On the other hand, the systematic recruitment of the dominant wealthy class came from the schools. Education took great strides as the evidence of school buildings, e.g., in Priene, of graffiti, papyri, and inscriptions, makes clear.

The changes in society produced a marked increase in individualism which was conspicuous also in the theater, while the stage came to reflect the actual focus of society—the bourgeois house. (See diagram below.) Tragedy continued to be played

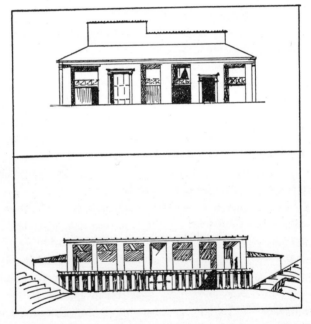

and, as was natural, Euripides took the place of favorite dramatist. But the innovations of the fourth century continued apace, and the creation of new tragedies yielded to the interpretation of old by great actors, who enjoyed large salaries and prestige, being even employed as ambassadors with diplomatic immunities. Their professional status was enhanced by the demand for performers at the festivals of the rich Hellenistic kings. The effects of scene painting were the model for court pleasure structures such as the tent of Ptolemy Philadelphus.[2] In this period a company on the road included not only tragedians and comedians but also musical *artistes,* whose individual performance in monodies took the place of the ancient chorus. A distinction grew up between thymelic contests and scenic, that is, of musical artists performing in the orchestra, and of dramatic artists performing on the high and narrow Hellenistic stage.[3] There arose a caste system among these professionals, for the Dionysiac companies were firm in excluding from their association the highly popular but rather disreputable performers of mime.

The drama which most accurately reflected contemporary upper-class society was the New Comedy of Menander, Diphilus, and Philemon.[4] Its scene was generally in Athens and its theme that of bourgeois romance. It was in effect a comedy of manners like that of Congreve, its lineal descendent upon the English stage. For its authors it was a kind of chess game within a range of forty-four standardized character masks, to which we shall return later in the concluding chapter.[5] Of these it shared some with the now standardized twenty-eight masks of tragedy; its three main classes of character were prosperous bourgeois, courtesans, and slaves. It is indeed a family drama, idealized like all Greek art, but dealing with the accidents which befall individuals, to whom Menander lends a charm not recognizable in Latin imitators of the New Comedy, except perhaps in Terence. Its variations have been wittily described by Post as almost algebraic, in a formula $w \dfrac{(x-y)}{z} = x+y,$ where $x-y$ represents the separated couple, z the dividing obstacle to their love and w the method of uniting them.[6] This drama is like the society it represented, civilized, rational, and articulate, not really comic in the broader sense so much as ironic and philosophic, compassionate and de-

tached. In Menander's considerable fragments the influence of
tragedy, especially later tragedy, is clearly traceable; indeed, the
effect which it produces on the reader is that of a slightly sentimental realism, a reflective drama which seems to fulfill the pre-
diction of Socrates in the *Symposium* of Plato, when he argues
against Aristophanes that the same men should be capable of
writing comedy and tragedy.[7] This well describes the work at
least of Menander, who is the only author of New Comedy on
whom we can form a judgment; for his plays are neither comedy
nor tragedy, they are romantic drama, in whose generalized tragi-
comic conflicts Tyche, the goddess of chance, plays a great role.
Its happy endings depend on accidents of recognition by which
hero and heroine are finally united on the discovery of lost birth
tokens proving her to be not a *fille de joie* but an Attic citizen. In
its atmosphere of slightly commercial pleasure it reflects the stand-
ards of a bourgeois Athens.

The close dependence of this comedy on Euripides was clear
even to antiquity. "All the gags about sudden dramatic change—
rape, substitution of babies, recognition by means of rings and
necklaces, all these are the stock in trade of New Comedy, and
were brought into prominence by Euripides," declares Satyros'
life of the tragedian.[8] In fact, both plot and even lines Menander
did not hesitate to take from the older dramatist. A comparison of
the *Ion* of Euripides and of Menander's *Girl with Shorn Hair*
will make this clearer.[9]

The *Ion* is one of the most realistic and, at the same time, ironic
of the Euripidean plays. At its conclusion little more is left of
the great symbolic Apollo of the *Eumenides* than the black-
guardly shadow of a name. The plot runs as follows: Creousa, a
princess of Athens, was violated by Apollo and bore a child,
which she laid in the cave where she had been ravished. The
child was taken by Apollo to Delphi, where he became sacristan
in the temple court. Creousa then married Xuthus, a rather rough-
and-ready, but generous, foreigner. Having no children, they went

to Delphi to inquire of the god about their prospects. At Delphi, Creousa meets Ion, and, liking him, tells him her story, stopping short of its climax. Xuthus, on inquiring of the god, is told that the first person he meets will be his son, a deceitful trick which is hardly worthy of a god. When Xuthus meets Ion and claims him as son, Ion is somewhat reluctant to assume the burdens of this unexpected paternity. He fends off Xuthus, who recalls how possibly he could have been his father. Ion objects to going to Athens and thinks that it would be unfair to Creousa. Xuthus says that he will adopt Ion and sets about preparing an adoption feast. The chorus, who overhear the whole discussion, are pledged to a vow of silence, which they promptly break on the arrival of Creousa with her old attendant male slave. Creousa thinks that Apollo is cheating her of her child and, maddened, plans revenge. The slave is to go and poison Ion at the feast. He fails, and Creousa takes refuge at the altar. The Delphic priestess now emerges from the temple with the birth tokens of Ion, a cloak embroidered with gorgons, a snake necklace, a sprig of olive, which reveals the identity of the boy. It is now Ion's turn to be angry; he wants to burn the temple down but is stopped, not by Apollo who is too ashamed, but by Athene, who restrains the angry child.

The recognition scene, a stage device of long standing from the *Choephoroe* onwards, is used in both the *Girl with Shorn Hair* of Menander and in his *Arbitrants,* which takes its title from an arbitration scene involving the birth tokens, also paralleled in a lost play of Euripides, the *Alope*. The handling of this recognition in the *Girl with Shorn Hair* closely follows the tragic pattern described above. The plot is as follows: Pataecus, father of two children, Glycera and Moschion, whom poverty had driven him to expose at birth, meeting Glycera when she is grown up, happens to see a dress of hers which arouses his suspicions. She shows him a chest which she has preserved, and, on recognizing the embroidery and necklace contained in it, he is finally convinced of her identity. In both plays the children require proof;

the necklace and robe are each time the means of identification; the parallels extend to similarities even of diction.[10] Thus, in the *Ion:*

> ION: What is the figure there? See thou deceive me not.
> CREOUSA: It is a gorgon woven in the midst of the warp.
> ION: Oh Zeus, what fate is this that tracks me!
> CREOUSA: Like to an aegis it is fringed with serpents.
> ION: Such is the woof and such the garment too.

Compare the play of Menander, where the lines preceding our quotation are missing. Pataecus and Glycera are examining the embroidery.

> PATAECUS: The same as I saw then. Isn't this next animal a goat or a bull or some such beast?
> GLYCERA: It's a stag, my friend, not a goat.
> PATAECUS: It has horns, that I know. And this third one is a winged horse. These things were the property of my wife, poor woman.

These contrasting scenes show curiously, even in translation, the increase of realism which constitutes their main difference. The gorgons of mythology give place to stags.

But if the realism of Menander is only one step further beyond Euripides, it is in the *Ion* also that we have a trace of the most realistic theatrical medium of the ancient stage, the mime, and we must return to pick up the thread of that secular Sicilian drama which we distinguished early in this study as the other distinctive form of the Greek theater besides the Attic. In the Hellenistic period, while the declension of tone was at work in Attic drama and a greater realism was emerging, the mime comes forth in our tradition from the shadow into which the prestige of the Attic theater had cast it. During this period there becomes obvious, in contrast to the narrowing circle of bourgeois interest, the greater scope which popular life afforded for dramatic representation. It is the drama of the rawer side of life, and its emergence is just as much a sign of the times as the radicalism of the philosophers already cited. Even among the educated reading public the works of the literary Theocritus and of Herodas show the ascension of the mime into the circle of court poets as a subject of fresh interest. It is unfortunate, therefore, that, while immensely popular and vigorous, a curious snobbery of ancient taste has prevented the survival of any of its scenarios, except two from Oxyrhynchus in Egypt which belong to Imperial times.[11] Like the *Commedia dell' arte* it must have owed much to topicality and improvisation, but with the aid of the Oxyrhynchus fragments and more respectable literary counterparts we may be able to reconstruct the main outline of its development. An interesting typology of characters and scenes is quite clear, and from a multitude of terra-cotta figures in the museums of Europe and America we can reconstruct some idea of how its characters appeared. It is the obverse side of the medal and the counterpart in the Hellenistic age to the bourgeois society of the New Comedy.

In discussing Attic Old Comedy we have already dealt with the new mythological figures who won a heartfelt response from the lower classes, chiefly the trickster Odysseus, the hungry Heracles, and the Cyclops. But from Epicharmus onwards to Theocritus and the Oxyrhynchus papyri we can trace the realistic note which indicates the closeness of this drama to everyday life. Among his titles Epicharmus has his *Temple Visitors, Fraudulent Soothsayers*, a *Victorious Athlete*, and a *Rustic; Sophron*, his *Isthmian Celebrators*, his *Moon-Invokers*, his *Tunnyfisher*, his *Fisher and Rustic*. A terra cotta of 300 B.C. from Athens shows a group from a mime entitled the *Mother-in-Law*.[12] Theocritus has his famous *Women at the Festival of Adonis*, his famous second *Idyll of the Girl Practising Magic*, his rustic workers in the field. Herodas has his *Women Offering Sacrifices to Asclepius, Women in Conversation, Bawd*, his *Brothel Keeper*, his *Cobbler*, his *Schoolmaster*, and his *Jealous Mistress*. The *Jealous Mistress* is the subject of one of the Oxyrhynchus fragments and is closely parallel to the literary mime of Herodas in the cruel punishments which the jealous woman inflicts on her unfaithful slave.[13] It is a revealing comment on a hidden side of ancient life.

The realism of the mime was in part due to the maskless, barefoot method of presentation. Unlike the masked and emphasized figures of what we may call the legitimate theater, the mime gave with perfect naturalism excerpts from the low but vigorous life of the age. Its vulgarity was a trend which naturally the upper-class drama rejected, but it is interesting to detect even in Euripides a raid upon its repertoire. In the same *Ion,* where his plot so clearly foreshadows the development of New Comedy, we have a scene taken over from the mimic typology. It was an ingenious method of treating the now superfluous chorus. He made them handmaids of Creousa but treated them as mimic ladies like the *Temple Visitors* of Epicharmus, or the *Women at the Feast of Adonis* of Theocritus, or those who in the mime of Herodas examine in detail the treasures of the precinct at Cos. In the *Ion* it is the hero himself who plays the role of guide and takes them on a tour of the temple, explaining the meaning of the sculptures. "I view it all attentively," they remark in chorus. "Observe the battle of the giants," continues the cicerone. "Let us note this, my friends," echoes the leader of this Intourist group.[14] In the treatment of the chorus, now an outworn survival of the original dramatic form, realism could no further go.

On the other hand, the larger Oxyrhynchus fragment very curiously reveals how closely Euripides caught the psychology of individualism. The dramatic form which he gave to that nostalgic *Sehnsucht,* that escapism which seems to appear in commercialized societies as a longing for far-off mysterious lands appears unexpectedly in the setting of this mimic play. It reads like a travesty of the *Iphigeneia in Tauris,* though both it and the Euripidean play may have had their origin in a popular tale. The heroine, Gracie, or Charition, is captive as priestess on a distant strand of India. Her speech, couched in fairly dignified language, is continually interrupted by the loud indecencies and the vulgar explosions of the mimic fool. She is planning escape for herself and her brother, and effects it by outwitting the king and his barbarian women, who jabber in Indian speech. They are made drunk with wine, and escape is easy. The whole fragment is punctuated by an obligato of kettledrums, indicated on the papyrus.

Thus ends the latest Greek play and the last mimic text. But it is interesting to note that even in these two chance fragments from Oxyrhynchus the mime remains true to type, for even in the *Jealous Mistress* and *Gracie* we see the last appearance of those twin strands of a popular comedy which began with Epicharmus, realism and mythological parody.

Chapter Six

SPECTACLE AND THOUGHT

A MONG the lesser of the five elements which Aristotle selects as essential to tragedy is spectacle, or, as we would term it today, the production. "While highly impressive, it is," he says, "quite alien to the art and has nothing to do with poetry. Indeed the effect of tragedy does not depend on its performance by actors, and, moreover, for achieving the spectacular the art of the producer is more important than that of the poet." [1]

From his own critical standpoint Aristotle is here perfectly right. Spectacle has nothing whatever to do with poetry. But it does have a lot to do with drama. It is an essential part of the psychological effect. Nowhere in the *Poetics* does Aristotle show more clearly than in these lines his literary conception of tragedy. But from our present point of view, which is that of a member of the audience and not of a critic in his study, the evidence which archaeology can furnish of the ancient manner of production cannot be disregarded. It is a unique check upon the truth of our conclusions, for if the reflection of society took the form we have suggested upon the ancient stage, then the link between the fictive lives of the actors and the lives of their audience must have been symbolized also in terms of costume, mask, and *décor* in a way quite intelligible to the spectators.

Here again, however, as in the language, ideas, and content of the plays we must draw a distinction between what would appeal to a primitive mind and what to a sophisticated one. We must make this note in advance. Psychologically the growth of visual imagination reverses that of verbal expression. The primitive mind, highly suggestible already and halfheartedly articulate, has no need of complex properties to supplement its own vivid power of creating symbols. Simple, intuitive, even naïve, it teems with them, and is extraordinarily alive visually. One recalls the recognition scene in the *Choephoroe* and the means of identification—the footstep, the lock of hair, the ancient robe—none of them proofs to a logical mind, but all of them excellent visual devices, even if Euripides in his day rejects them for his own Electra with deliberate parody. This visual power is the complement of primitive speech, which is highly colorful, complex, and pregnant with meaning. Just as a ceremonial elaboration still clothes the words of Pindar, the "great bull words" of Aeschylus, to use Aristophanes' phrase,[2] are compounds of ideas rushing together in a cloudy articulation. On the other hand, the reverse holds good for a more sophisticated age. Speech then aims above all at clarity and a clear-cut sharpness, while visually the lessened suggestibility which accompanies an increase of consciousness and power of verbal expression requires as offset the stimulus of illusion or display to move an inhibited imagination.

If, then, we intend to use the visual appearance of the stage to corroborate the change in thought from mythological to logical processes, we must expect to find a powerful symbolism speaking directly to the primitive mind; and, to the more conscious, either sensationalism or a realism which depends for its deceptive truth to nature upon a skillfully combined and consciously recognizable art. Further, if, as we have found in the mythological content of plot, there is a gradual increase in secularization and a growing tendency to replace the symbol with reality, then we shall expect a more secular note also in the *décor*. Finally, if the ultimate fate of tragedy and comedy was to be fused in the creation of a bourgeois drama, as we have maintained, the proof of this view must extend as well to the appearance of the characters. It must be reflected visibly not only in similarity of acting types but also in clothing and masks. With these provisos then in mind, we may now examine the material of the Greek theater. This falls under two headings—stage setting, or *décor,* and the actors.

Into the long and bitterly fought battle of the Greek stage it is a brave man who ventures with a new theory. Such certainly is not the purpose of the following paragraphs. Rather is it to extract from the welter of conflicting evidence the salient facts which are explicable in social terms. Three periods concern us— the archaic, the later fifth century, and the Hellenistic. In each of these periods the drama was played against a different setting, and in each also social considerations have a bearing on its evolution. The first is that of the dominant chorus, the second of the chorus in decline, the third of two distinct performances—that in the orchestra of musical artists, the thymelic, and that of the actors upon the stage, the scenic. They correspond politically to the transition from tribal aristocracy to democracy, to the period of democracy, and to that of a bourgeois Athens; in other words, from Peisistratus to Cimon, from Pericles to the Thirty Tyrants, from Demetrius of Phaleron to the coming of the Romans.

In the first period (534–465 B.C.) the chorus moved freely in the orchestra with little behind it to distract the eye, in the second (465–404 B.C.) an experimental background gradually took permanent shape, in the third (317–86 B.C.) a quite new conception of dramatic setting was in vogue.[3] We must be content with grouping the established essentials of the changes rather than the disputed detail, but, before beginning an account of it, we must remember that in so conservative an atmosphere as the Greek theater the change was at no time sudden, but the result of a long and careful testing. The theater for the Greeks was primarily an open-air place of assembly for the community as a whole, and in communities like Priene, for example, which had no open-air Pnyx, as at Athens, for its political meetings, it was *the* assembly place par excellence, and its tiers of seating the fairly logical plan for smaller, roofed-in halls, which in Priene, as elsewhere, are a feature of Hellenistic city architecture.[4]

It is worth noting that in the archaic period the celebrations of the Dionysiac festivals originated not in the precinct of the god on the southern slopes of the Acropolis but in the Agora, or public square. They were later moved to what became the theater, for the rising hillside provided a better view for the spectators. As one would expect, the theater at this time was not a theater at all in the later sense of a stage and auditorium. It was only a circular dancing place or orchestra near the temple of the god, built around 600 B.C. (see p. 14). This orchestra was approached by a forking road which led up to it from the altar. It continued thus until the beginning of the fifth century, and the few accessories of the earlier Aeschylean plays reflect this setting.[5] The *Suppliants* has a group of shrines to the Twelve Gods to represent the Agora at Argos, an arrangement similar to that of the Agora in Athens, where the festival had once been held. Hence, in lieu of setting we have symbolism which is elaborated in the address of the Suppliants. As the background of the *Seven,* Aeschylus again makes use of the statues of the gods ranged round the center of the Theban citadel. In each of these plays he reinforces the symbolism of the *décor,* with frequent references to a lesser symbolism—in the *Suppliants* to the "white crowned wands of suppliance," the wool tufted branches which they carry, in the *Seven* with the elaborately sketched symbolism of the shields of the seven champions.[6] In both plays the center of movement was the altar in the middle of the orchestra. In the *Persians* the tomb of Dareius on the edge of the orchestra was a symbol of the fallen hopes of Persia. Above it emerged the ghost of Dareius; in the *Prometheus* it served for the rock against which the hero is chained and behind which he crashes over the stone parapet out of sight.

In the *Oresteia* symbolism is used magnificently to enhance a growing elaboration of the setting. In the crimson robe which Clytemnestra flings down before Agamemnon, in the same crimson robe in which she herself is murdered, again in the crimson robes which the Eumenides wear at their departure, we have a reiterative appeal to the visual mentality.[7] The setting of the *Oresteia* represents, like that of the *Ajax* of Sophocles, an advance in *décor*. In 465 B.C., seven years previously, the dancing place had been moved back to permit the erection of a storage hall lying athwart the orchestra, whose permanent form of uncertain date was a long barn (see p. 20) with a blank face turned to the audience and a central door. The roof was more probably flat than sloping as in the restoration, for on it walked in the light of the breaking day the Watchman of the *Agamemnon*. Slits in its surface permitted variation of effects. In the *Oresteia* (see p. 29) they represented the projecting columnar propylon of the palace at Mycenae, then Apollo's temple at Delphi, and, finally, the entrance to the Acropolis with the court of the Areopagus in front in the orchestra. This columnar effect must have been quite simple, not at all dissimilar to the Peisistratid entrance to the Acropolis which was perhaps its inspiration (see p. 30). It likewise consisted of a columned porch breaking a long line of walls. Since the line of the new storehouse shut off the landscape view around the temple of Dionysus, the illusion of a landscape setting could now be restored only by one means—scene painting with spatial suggestion. The invention of this is attributed to Sophocles. We can judge fairly accurately of the nature of such scene painting from the spatial effects that now begin in the vase painting. Although Agatharchus is credited at this period with the discovery of perspective, the suggestion of space must have been still very limited and, as in the vases, largely symbolic— a ship's prow or dolphin for the shore, a prim little row of trees and a rock for a *paysage,* but psychologically the attempt makes a transition to a more consciously suggestive mentality in the audience.

For acoustic reasons also it was found simpler to adopt a standard arrangement which took shape near the end of the century (*c.*420–400 B.C.) in the form of a stone skene with a projecting wing at either end (see p. 32). The resultant effect was of a court with three sides, open to the orchestra. It permitted variable arrangements between the two wings and an upper story, on which the gods made their appearance. It could be used to show three separate houses, as in the *Frogs* of Aristophanes. Again the general appearance must on occasion have borne more than a coincidental likeness to the Periclean propylaea, which in both the *Lysistrata* and *Women at the Thesmophoria* of Aristophanes is the actual background of the play (see p. 47).

The Hellenistic skene (see p. 62), like its drama, was a different matter. In the lower story, surrounded with a paneled colonnade of acoustic wood, the side wings became practically rudimentary, projecting only slightly at each end. The thymelic, or musical, performances continued to be held in the orchestra, but dramatic action, now divorced from the chorus, went on at a higher level in front of large openings in the background. These should be compared with the house front of a characteristic Hellenistic house in Pompeii in the same diagram. With such a setting the stage could easily be converted into the illusion of a street with several houses, the standard setting of the New Comedy. At the same time the suggestion of an interior could be given by the use of screens (see the illustration on the next page), again almost identical with the actual interior of the Hellenistic house, where screens were used in the large central hall. An alternative landscape setting was made possible by an advancing perspective, and revolving prisms, or *periaktoi,* permitted a change of scene between plays.[8]

Thus, just as the drama kept pace with a changing society, the setting for the spectacle of the Greek stage was subject also to the same influences. At each period realism and symbolism made themselves felt in varying proportion. And at each period the setting reflected the forms of social interest at the time. In the

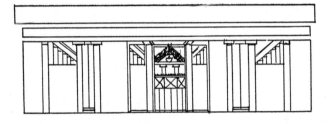

archaic, when religious influence was strongest, the background of the drama is realistically the dancing place with its altar before the temple of the god; the drama itself is reinforced by a simple but powerful symbolism in its accessories. In the middle fifth century the Dionysiac shrine is hidden by the storehouse of the state festival. The setting becomes a simple, symbolical façade interchangeably temple or palace gateway, which recall the buildings of the city-state, while scene painting brings with it a more conscious attempt at illusive realism. In the Hellenistic period symbolism practically disappears, and for the realistic representation of a row of bourgeois houses can be substituted an artistic realism with considerable truth to nature. Thus the *décor* reflects alike the society of the time and its psychology.

The same evolution is traceable in the costume and masks. Again we find the same origins and the same conservatism. The task of Aeschylus, here again the creative genius, was to lend dignity to the new secular drama. He started accordingly from the ritual elements to which public opinion already attached considerable sanctity. Thus, both in the dance movements which he extemporized to suit the new medium on the models of the old religious forms, and also in the costumes and masks, he was an innovator and secularizer in terms of the existing religion. We have already seen in the *Eumenides* how successfully he embodied in terms of the popular imagination these spirits of the tribal law. So also in the tragic costume he started from the old-fashioned Ionian ceremonial costume.[9] The long-sleeved, flowered robe was the garment of Dionysus himself in his old cult forms, as too of the hierophants of Aeschylus' native Eleusis, from which Athenaeus tells us he borrowed it.[10] Here again, however, he blended secular innovations, for along with the religious source he chose as well from another, which reflected the history of the city-state. This was the oriental splendor of the Persians whom Athens had defeated [11] (see headpiece to this chapter). Just as the Odeion of Pericles was built from the loot of the Persian ships, so Aeschylus took the rich garments and Persian tiara of the Orient as colorful symbols of royalty. But, here again, with the increase of consciousness realism also crept in. If the Medea of Euripides still appears like a gorgeous figure of the East, there is contrast in the realistic rags of Telephus, while his Electra appears like a down-at-heel country woman, to whom the chorus are ready to lend a few trinkets to mend her appearance. In the Hellenistic period the flowered robe of Dionysus fits easily and appropriately on the shoulders of the bourgeois procurer of New Comedy.

The Hellenistic masks which Pollux describes in such detail are shown by the surviving copies of them in terra cottas or sculpture to have been intensified, almost sensational, variants of the older types [12] (see headpiece to Chap. V). The great *onkos,* or headdress, of this period achieves the same effect of adding height which the tiara of Oriental royalty achieved in earlier times (see

headpiece to this chapter and accompanying illustration); the *speira,* or conventionalized roll of hair, which marks the leading characters of New Comedy is a survival of an archaic Doric method of dressing the hair.[13] But it is in the contrast of the tragic and comic masks of Pollux that we find confirmation of what we earlier surmised of the relationship of New Comedy to Euripidean tragedy, for in both categories we find a parallelism in the more romantic characters. In both we find the *kore,* or maiden; the *pseudokore,* or maiden in distress, has her counterpart in tragedy; among the young men the adventurous "good for all work," the "lad with crisp locks," the "lad with the delicate air," are found in each drama. Even in appearance, as the terra cottas prove, they must have been surprisingly alike upon the stage.[14] For in contrast to the earlier comic masks which Aristotle rightly found so ugly, those of the New Comedy heroes and heroines are marked by that serene idealism which always distinguishes Greek sculpture.[15] Some of the older masks for slave characters the New Comedy retained—traditional ones like the Megarian slave, Maison, the cook of New Comedy.

Thus, New Comedy both in content and in appearance was a fusion of fifth-century dramatic forms that corresponded to a leveling process in a bourgeois society. It was the mime which became the expression of the older democratic realism, even in its most intensified form. Here again the drama was symptomatic of a shift of social interest. For the radical trends of the age took expression in a realism that affected literature, drama, and sculpture alike, as in the terra cotta of the mimic fool below.

NOTES

Chapter One

1. G. Thomson, "The Social Origins of Greek Tragedy," *Modern Quarterly,* I (1938), 233–64. See also his *Aeschylus and Athens* (London, 1941).

2. The best treatment of myth as a feature of primitive thought is that of B. Malinowski, *Myth in Primitive Psychology* (London, 1926). Though the material is drawn from the Melanesians, the essay is highly suggestive, and its principles may be applied with reservation, *mutatis mutandis,* to the primitive period of Greek culture.

3. Plutarch *Themistocles* xiii and v.

4. W. Jaeger, *Paideia,* translated by G. Highet (Oxford, 1939), p. 244.

Chapter Two

1. Aristotle *Poetics* iv, v. 1449a–b.

2. For the long history of the mime see A. Nicoll, *Masks, Mimes, and Miracles* (London, 1931); for the classical period, pp. 20–134.

3. For the South Italian comedy see M. Bieber, *History of the Greek and Roman Theater* (Princeton, 1939), pp. 258–300; for the influence of the mime and South Italian comedy on Plautus see my article in "Harvard Studies in Classical Philology," XLIX (1938), 205–28. For the fragments of the mime see A. Olivieri, *Frammenti della commedia greca e del mimo nella Sicilia e nella Magna Grecia* (Naples, 1930).

4. The chief theories of the ritual origin in Greek tragedy are summarized with bibliography in Bieber, *op. cit.,* p. 7; for criticism of them see A. W. Pickard-Cambridge, *Dithyramb, Tragedy, and Comedy* (Oxford, 1927); for the latest theory, namely, origin in the ritual of the totemic clan see Thomson, *Aeschylus and Athens,* pp. 97–196.

5. M. Pohlenz, *Die griechische Tragödie* (Leipzig, 1930), p. 7.

6. *Ibid.,* p. 4.

7. *Theognis,* ll. 53–56.

8. Solon *Elegy* III (Diehl).

9. For Periander and Cleisthenes see Herodotus i.23; v.67.

10. See Thomson, *op. cit.*, pp. 151–52, 194–95.

11. Herodotus i.60.

12. E. A. Gardner and M. Cary in *The Cambridge Ancient History*, III, 585–86.

13. P. Vinogradoff, *Outlines of Historical Jurisprudence* (Oxford, 1922), II, 85.

14. See Malinowski, *Crime and Custom in Savage Society* (London, 1932), for emphasis on the dynamic as opposed to the inhibitive features of primitive law among the Melanesians.

15. L. H. Morgan, *Ancient Society* (Chicago, 1907), pp. 221–84.

16. *Ibid.*, p. 228.

17. See W. S. Ferguson, "The Athenian Phratries," *Classical Philology*, V (1910), 257–84.

18. Such evidence as there is in Greek mythology for totemism has been collected by Thomson, *op. cit.*, pp. 19–20; for the question of matrilineal descent see Chap. III, below, and Thomson, *op. cit.*, pp. 28–31, 51, 120, 277–79.

19. See Ferguson, *op. cit.*, pp. 264–65.

20. V. Pareto, *Trattato di sociologia generale.* 3 vols. (Florence, 1923).

Chapter Three

1. Aeschylus *Eumenides*, ll. 653–56. (Sidgwick).

2. *Ibid.*, ll. 658–61.

3. Thomson, *Aeschylus and Athens*, pp. 29, 277.

4. Aeschylus *Eumenides*, ll. 734–38.

5. Euripides *Orestes*, ll. 551–60 (Murray), 602–4.

6. Aristotle *De generatione animalium* iv; for Hippocratic influence on Euripides see W. Nestlé, *Der Dichter der griechischen Aufklärung* (Stuttgart, 1901), pp. 99, 170–73.

7. For Phrynichus and Pratinas see Pickard-Cambridge, *Dithyramb, Tragedy, and Comedy*, pp. 90–97.

8. Pohlenz, *Die griechische Tragödie*, p. 54.

9. See Thomson's edition of the *Oresteia* (Cambridge, 1938), pp. 11–12.

10. W. Ridgeway, *Origin of Tragedy* (Cambridge, 1910), p. 190.

11. Justin, ii.6; Varro, ap. Augustine *De civitate dei* xviii.9.

12. See Pohlenz, *op. cit.*, p. 92.

13. Aeschylus *Agamemnon*, ll. 176–9 (Sidgwick).

14. Solon *Elegy* i.33–36 (Diehl).

15. Aeschylus *Agamemnon*, ll. 763–68.

16. Solon *Elegy* i.25–32 (Diehl).

17. Malinowski, *Crime and Custom in Savage Society*, pp. 94–95, 97.

18. Aeschylus *Choephoroe*, ll. 402–4 (Sidgwick); for an excellent exposition of the emotional effect of this *kommos*, ll. 306–478 see Thomson's *Oresteia*, I, 37.

19. Sir R. C. Jebb, *Trachiniae* (Cambridge, 1892), Introduction, pp. xxiii–xxv.

Chapter Four

1. Cratinus *Comicorum graecorum fragmenta*, ed. Kock, 307.

2. Plutarch *Glory of the Athenians* v.

3. T. Zielinski, *Die Gliederung der altattischen Komödie*, (Leipzig, 1885).

4. E. O'Neill, Jr., in the Introduction to the section on comedy in W. J. Oates and E. O'Neill, Jr., *The Complete Greek Drama* (New York, 1938), p. xl.

5. See Bieber, *History of the Greek and Roman Theater*, Figs. 110–17. Fig. 117, described as "a parody of a king," may well represent Dionysus himself wearing the long-sleeved garment typical of him.

6. Aeschylus *Choephoroe*, ll. 164–234 (Sidgwick); Euripides *Electra*, ll. 487–584 (Murray).

Chapter Five

1. The mime figures are well represented in Hellenistic terra cottas. For types representative of the street life of Hellenistic cities see M. Rostovtzeff's *Social and Economic History of the Hellenistic World* (Oxford, 1941), I, 176, Plate XXV; 212, Plate XXX; 239, Plate XXXIII; 246, Plate XXXIV; 416, Plate L.

2. See F. Studniczka, "Das Symposion Ptolemaios II," *Kön. Sachs. Gesellschaft d. Wissensch., Abhandl. philol. hist. Klasse*, XXX, No. 2 (1914), 4–188. For the adoption of scene painting to decorate the interior of the Hellenistic house see my articles, "The Decoration of the Hellenistic Peristyle House in South Italy," in *American Journal of Archaeology*, XXXIX (1935), 360–71, and "Scaenographia," in *Art Bulletin*, XVIII (1936), 407–18.

3. For the Hellenistic performance see T. Birt, *Die Schaubauten der Griechen und die attische Tragödie* (Berlin, 1931), pp. 19–20.

4. See C. R. Post, "The Dramatic Art of Menander," *Harvard Studies in Classical Philology,* XXIV (1913), 111–45.

5. The masks are described by Pollux in his *Onomasticon* iv.133–54 and are fully discussed with reference to the archaeological material by C. Robert, *Winckelmannsprogramm* 25 (Halle, 1911); compare Bieber, *History of the Greek and Roman Theater,* pp. 163–205.

6. Post, *op. cit.,* p. 112.

7. Plato *Symposium* 223d.

8. Satyros *Life of Euripides* in H. von Arnim, *Supplementum Euripideum* (Bonn, 1913), p. 5.

9. For the similarities of Menander and Euripides see M. Andrewes, "Euripides and Menander," *Classical Quarterly,* XVIII (1924), 1–10.

10. Euripides *Ion,* ll. 1420–24 (Murray); Menander *Perikeiromene,* ll. 646–51 (Allinson).

11. B. P. Grenfell and A. S. Hunt, *Oxyrhynchus Papyri* (London, 1903), III, 41–57.

12. Bieber, *op. cit.,* p. 204, Fig. 290.

13. For interpretation of this fragment see O. Crusius, *Herondae mimiambi* (Leipzig, 1914), pp. 110–16.

14. Euripides *Ion,* ll. 205–7.

Chapter Six

1. Aristotle *Poetics* VI, 1450b.

2. Aristophanes *Frogs,* l. 924.

3. For the history of the stage building in the first two periods see Bieber, *History of the Greek and Roman Theater,* Chap. V, "The Development of the Theater Building in the Classical Period," pp. 99–162; for the last period, Chap. IX, "The Hellenistic Theater Building," pp. 206–57.

4. For theater-like buildings in Hellenistic architecture at Priene and Miletus see D. S. Robertson, *Greek and Roman Architecture* (Cambridge, 1929), pp. 176–80.

5. The settings of the individual plays of Aeschylus are enumerated by A. Frickenhaus, *Die altgriechische Bühne* (Strassburg, 1917), pp. 4, 11, 12.

6. For the symbolism of the Suppliants' wands Aeschylus *Suppliants,* ll. 21–22, 506; for that of the Champions' shields, *Seven against Thebes,* ll. 387–594 (Sidgwick).

7. The symbolism of the crimson robe is stressed by Thomson, *Oresteia,* Introduction, pp. 67–69.

8. For the scenery of the Hellenistic stage see Bieber, *op. cit.,* pp. 248–52, and my article, "Scaenographia," *Art Bulletin,* XVIII (1936), 407–18.

9. For the ceremonial robe, Bieber, *op. cit.,* pp. 37–40, Fig. 42.

10. Athenaeus *Deipnosophistae* i.21e.

11. The figure of Aietes, father of Medea, taken from the Medea Vase in Munich (Bieber, *op. cit.,* Fig. 72), shows on its head the Persian tiara, or cap, which the Greeks took as typical headgear for the Oriental monarch.

12. For the costumes and masks of New Comedy see Bieber, *op. cit.,* pp. 163–205, Figs. 223–89.

13. Comparison of the headpiece to Chapter VI and the Pompeian wall painting of the actor as king dedicating his mask reveals the persistence in tragic costume of the long-sleeved robe, the broad sash, the eagle-crowned scepter, and the origin of the *onkos* with its long, straggling locks in the curling tiara of the Oriental fifth-century king; for the origin of the *speira* see Bieber, *op. cit.,* p. 189, and compare Fig. 41.

14. See Bieber, *loc. cit.,* Figs. 204–5, 207, 230.

15. Aristotle *Poetics* v., 1449a.

BIBLIOGRAPHY

THE FOLLOWING BIBLIOGRAPHY comprises modern works used in the preparation of the text. Ancient authorities are cited in the notes.

Andrewes, M. "Euripides and Menander," *Classical Quarterly,* XVIII (1924), 1–10.

Arnim, H. von. *Supplementum Euripideum.* Bonn, 1913.

Bieber, M. *The History of the Greek and Roman Theater.* Princeton, 1939.

Birt, T. *Die Schaubauten der Griechen und die attische Tragödie.* Berlin, 1931.

Crusius, O. *Herondae mimiambi.* Leipzig, 1914.

Ferguson, W. S. "The Athenian Phratries," *Classical Philology,* V, 1910, 257–84.

Fiechter, E. R. *Das Dionysos-theater in Athen.* Stuttgart, 1935–36.

Frickenhaus, A. *Die altgriechische Bühne.* Strassburg, 1917.

Gardner, E. A., and M. Cary, in *Cambridge Ancient History,* III, Chap. XXIII, "Early Athens," 571–97.

Grenfell, B. P., and A. S. Hunt. *Oxyrhynchus Papyri.* Vol. III. London, 1903.

Jaeger, W. *Paideia.* Translated by G. Highet. Oxford, 1939.

Jebb, R. C. *The Trachiniae of Sophocles.* Cambridge, 1892.

Kock, T. *Comicorum atticorum fragmenta.* Leipzig, 1880–88.

Little, A. M. G. "The Decoration of the Hellenistic Peristyle House in South Italy," *American Journal of Archaeology,* XXXIX (1935), 360–71.

——— "Scaenographia," *Art Bulletin,* XVIII (1936), 407–18.

——— "Plautus and Popular Comedy," *Harvard Studies in Classical Philology,* XLIX (1938), 205–38.

Malinowski, B. *Myth in Primitive Psychology.* London, 1926.

——— *Crime and Custom in Savage Society.* London, 1932.

Morgan, L. H. *Ancient Society.* Chicago, 1907.

Murray, G. *Euripides and His Age.* New York, 1913.

——— *Aristophanes, a Study.* New York, 1933.

88   *Bibliography*

Nestlé, W. *Der Dichter der griechischen Aufklärung.* Stuttgart, 1901.

Nicoll, A. *Masks, Mimes, and Miracles.* London, 1931.

Oates, W. J., and E. O'Neill, Jr. *The Complete Greek Drama.* New York, 1938.

Olivieri, A. *Frammenti della commedia greca e del mimo nella Sicilia e nella Magna Grecia.* Naples, 1930.

Pareto, V. *Trattato di sociologia generale.* Florence, 1923. 3 vols.

Pickard-Cambridge, A. W. *Dithyramb, Tragedy, and Comedy.* Oxford, 1927.

Pohlenz, M. *Die griechische Tragödie.* Leipzig, 1930.

Post, C. R. "The Dramatic Art of Menander," *Harvard Studies in Classical Philology,* XXIV (1913), 111–45.

Ridgeway, W. *The Origin of Tragedy.* Cambridge, 1910.

Robert, C. "Die Masken, der neueren attischen Komödie," in *Winckelmannsprogramm 25.* Halle, 1911.

Robertson, D. S. *Greek and Roman Architecture.* Cambridge, 1929.

Rostovtzeff, M. *The Social and Economic History of the Hellenistic World.* Oxford, 1941.

Studniczka, F. "Das Symposion Ptolemaios II." Königliche Sachsische Gesellschaft der Wissenschaften, Abhandlungen der philologisch-historischen Klasse, XXX, No. 2 (1914), 4–188.

Thomson, G. "The Social Origins of Greek Tragedy." *Modern Quarterly,* I (1938).

—— *Aeschylus,* Oresteia. Cambridge, 1938.

—— *Aeschylus and Athens.* London, 1941.

Vinogradoff, P. *Outlines of Historical Jurisprudence.* Oxford, 1920–22. 2 vols.

Zielinski, T. *Die Gliederung der altattischen Komödie.* Leipzig, 1885.

INDEX